We Are Not as Ethical as We Think We Are

Conversations about Low Visibility Decisions that Corrupt Government, Business and Ourselves

or

Better Ethical Conduct in Six Steps

D1569191

by

Jay Albanese, Ph.D.

ISBN-13: 978-1-7333004-2-1

Great Ideas Publishing
An imprint of McMaster Media
21010 Southbank Street - 550
Potomac Falls, Virginia 20165

Library of Congress Control Number: 2020945133

Albanese, Jay S.
We Are Not as Ethical as We Think We Are
Printed in the United States of America on acid-free paper
Second Printing

Synopsis

Books can be considered lectures, and lectures are overrated. No one talking at you for an entire book is that interesting. Conversations are much more interesting and memorable. This is a book of conversations about personal decisions to behave in ethical or unethical ways. Of course, we all tend to think that we behave ethically most of the time, and there is some evidence to support this. On the other hand, few of us behave ethically as much as we should, and none of us behaves ethically all the time. That's right. None of us.

The conversations recounted here help to understand the ethical conditions around us, and our own decisions, concerning matters large and small. As a university professor, I talk with students for a living. It is a good life, because nothing is better than talking about important ideas (other than acting on them)!

These conversations talk about good conduct, where it comes from, and why we don't see it more often in daily life. Bad conduct is featured in the headlines every day. Why isn't ethical conduct more common among those who act on behalf of others? (e.g., public and business officials.) In six compelling chapters, this book recounts conversations between me and my students that reveal answers to the most important questions of all: what is ethical, why doesn't it occur more often, and how can we improve ethical conduct in our personal and public life?

One of the best ways to think out loud is through a conversation. Thoughtful conversations about ethics can help move us toward principled action. All the characters in this book are composites of students the author has known, but the events are real. I hope these conversations about ethics are as enlightening for you as they were for me.

DEDICATION

*To all those who, like me, search for meaning
in everyday life, only to find it
in conversations about important ideas, like ethics*

CONTENTS

We Are Not as Ethical as We Think We Are

INTRODUCTION

"You undoubtedly think you are more ethical than you really are!" I declared this in my opening comments in a new course on ethics.

"Oh, really?" said Kelsey, a student sitting in the front row.

"Yes, in fact, global survey data indicate that most people believe that," added Johnny, a student sitting next to Kelsey.

"But those are anonymous survey respondents, not real people like me," chimed in Maria, a student sitting in the rear.

"O.K., let's see how ethical you are," I continued. "Let's say you go to the drug store to pick up a prescription from your physician. The charge is $10. You hand the 18-year-old cashier, wearing a 'new employee' tag, a $20 bill, expecting $10 back in change. Instead, the new cashier, clearly struggling with the digital cash register, hands you $40 cash. It quickly becomes obvious to you that she mistook your $20 bill for a $50 bill---resulting in giving you $30 in too much change."

"What a bonus!" said Johnny.

"Two questions should come immediately to your mind," I added:
(1) do you realize this is an ethical dilemma, and
(2) what do you do with the $30 overpayment to you?"

Johnny replied, "It's the drug store's fault, the cashier's fault, and the store overcharges anyway on a range of its products."

"Aren't those after-the-fact excuses, Johnny?" asked Kelsey.

"Those are rationalizations for theft," added Maria.

"Yes," I replied. "Your first reaction in this situation should be: 'this is an ethical dilemma, which requires me to make an ethical decision!' Recognition of ethical dilemmas when we see them is lacking in most people, because ethical principles are not included in much of primary, secondary, or university education."

"Are you saying that most people do not realize that placing the blame on the store or the employee is a rationalization for unethical and corrupt conduct?" asked Maria, from the back row.

"So what should I do in this situation?" I said, asking no one in particular.

Maria asserted her view: "A straightforward application of ethical principles would lead to an easy decision: you have no right to the $30 overpayment. The excess money does not belong to you."

"There are consequences to your actions, including the possible firing of the employee when the cash register does not balance at the end of the day," added Kelsey.

"Well, you might be right, but that's not a difficult decision to make," Johnny concluded.

I replied to them, "But it is an important decision, because ethical decisions are made every day in government, business, and personal life, and they often are made incorrectly (and unethically). In almost every case we will consider, a person does not appreciate that the conduct is wrong, nor are the consequences or harm of that conduct considered objectively."

Maria said, "There's also the problem of a self-serving bias. The position you are in influences the way you judge facts."

What do you mean?' asked Kelsey.

"There's a lot of experience that shows what Maria says is true," I observed. "A study was done involving reporting the details of a car accident. It found that the facts of the case were evaluated differently, depending on whether a person was assigned the role of the plaintiff or the defendant in the case" (Lowenstein, 1993).

"In another case I read about," added Johnny, "judgments about whether or not the actions of government agents constituted the torture of terrorism suspects were different, depending on whether or not the alleged misconduct was carried by in-country government agents, or agents outside your home country" (Tarrant, 2012).

Maria concluded, "So your role or position in a situation can bias your evaluation of facts, leading to unethical decisions, even though you are acting sincerely."

I added, "Knowing ethical principles, and how to apply them objectively, work against unconscious bias in assessing facts."

Johnny made an important related point. "The harm caused by corruption often occurs far from the person who makes the unethical decision---and sometimes far in the future."

"How's that?" asked Kelsey.

"I have an example," said Maria. "A drug dealer sells illicit drugs to others on a consensual basis, but in one case the drug sold causes the death of the buyer. Should the drug dealer be held responsible for the death?"

"No," said Kelsey. "The buyer engaged in a voluntary exchange."

"I disagree," said Johnny. "The seller created the situation that permitted the harm to occur, so the drug dealer is responsible."

"Distance from the victim often conceals your role in creating the harm," I noted. "If there is any uncertainty over whether your personal conduct is directly responsible for a bad outcome, it reduces your feeling of moral responsibility" (Falk & Szech, 2013; Hamman, Lowenstein & Weber, 2010).

"If we make ethics a personal matter, rather an abstract one, it helps to reduce this distance," I concluded.

"Relying on actual case studies is one way to draw a direct line between actions and harms," Johnny added.

I proposed, "So where do we begin to make more ethical decisions, more often?"

"It seems that knowing ethical principles, applying them objectively, while not discounting the potential harms we cause, are all important to consider," answered Kelsey.

"The first step is to overcome ignorance of ethical principles," said Maria, "which somehow are on the sidelines in modern education."

"If I learn the ethical principles, will I be ethical?" asked Kelsey.

"No, that's always a *choice* you make," I replied. "But knowing the principles removes a primary argument we often hear."

"And that argument is what?" asked Johnny.

"Ignorance."

"Yes, we'll take away the largest excuse of all!" Johnny added.

CHAPTER 1

Ignorance vs. Knowledge:
Knowing ethical principles

I was sitting at the gate of Los Angeles International Airport heading home, but there was a flight delay. You know the situation: as the original departure-time gets closer, and then it passes, the passengers draw closer and closer to the gate, and the grumbling gets louder, as people complain openly to no one in particular.

"They crowd closer to the gate as if they could *will* the plane to arrive or depart!" added Johnny.

"And some consider storming the gate, running down the jet-way and off the edge into nothingness," I added.

Kelsey noted, "You've seen way too many airport movies!"

I continued, "Even the flight crew and flight attendants were hovered in a group near the gate, looking at their phones, and observing the sad and unruly condition of the passengers they would soon be serving."

"At one point the gate agent makes an announcement, 'if you have bags on the seat next to you here at the gate, please remove them so other folks can sit down during this delay.'"

"So that's what I did. I put all my stuff on the floor in front of me, and someone came over and sat in that seat next to me," I said.

"Why did you have your stuff in that seat in the first place?" asked Kelsey.

"When I first got there no one was around, so I wasn't paying attention," I replied weakly.

"So you had no real excuse?" Maria added.

"Precisely. But the flight eventually took off, and I had an aisle seat with a completely full flight of unhappy people who were now behind schedule," I noted.

"Yes, the passengers were probably unhappy because mechanical problems on the plane were rudely placed ahead of their personal schedules!" said Johnny.

"Pretty much," said Kelsey and Maria simultaneously.

I continued, "An hour or so into the flight, the flight attendants came around to offer drinks and food (for purchase only---yes, I was in economy class---once again!). It was a long flight to DC, so I was thinking carefully about the drinks. But before I could say anything, the flight attendant says, 'What drink can I buy for you?'"

"Buy ME a drink?"

"Yes, I'm getting you whatever you want at no charge," she replied.

"Are you sure you aren't dreaming?" The thought crossed my mind, so I asked the flight attendant again, "Are you sure?"

The flight attendant replied, "Yes, when this flight was detained at the gate, you recall an announcement was made for people to move their stuff off chairs so other folks could sit down?"

"Yes, I remember."

"Well, I was watching, and you were the only person who moved their stuff to create an open seat. I want to thank you for that."

"I'll have a gin and tonic," I replied.

"Here are two bottles of gin," she responded. "You might need a second."

I thanked her, and she left.

"What kind of gin was it?"

"Why can I always count on my students to ask the most important questions?" I observed. "For the record, it was Bombay Sapphire."

"Nice!" the students said in unison.

I added, "There was a time when students did not know the differences between gins. There was the cheapest (which we always bought), and then there was everything else."

"We've learned to experience life a little more fully than in your day," said Johnny.

"So is there a moral to this story, beyond 'be nice and you might get free gin?'" asked Maria.

"Pay attention to airport gate announcements?" asked Kelsey.

"It's important to respect the legitimate interests of others, and failure to do so is at the base of unethical behavior," I said.

Maria said enthusiastically, "Yes! Having an ethical outlook has little value, unless it is accompanied by the willingness to *act* ethically."

* * * * * * *

"This leads us to a crucial point," I acknowledged. "Many people are ignorant of ethical principles, and knowledge of them is the first step toward becoming an ethical person."

"Some have said that corruption is the largest problem in the world," Maria inserted into the conversation.

"Corruption and ethics are closely related. Corruption is indeed a very serious problem, but it is number 2 on the list," I replied. "Ignorance is the largest problem in the world. Ignorance, which is the lack of knowledge or awareness of facts, is a more fundamental problem. Corruption is the misuse of position or trust, but it implies knowledge (a lack of ignorance) of what those responsibilities are."

"How are corruption and ethics related?" asked Johnny.

"Unethical behavior lies at the root of all corrupt conduct," replied Kelsey.

"We can't say it any better than that!" I responded.

Maria added, "I remember the quote from Socrates, 'Anyone who holds a true opinion without understanding is like a blind man on the right road'" (Plato, *Republic*, 505c).

"Yes," I replied. "Holding opinions without knowledge blinds us on our journey through life, which makes ignorance the fundamental problem. Ignorance impedes our ability to determine the facts for ourselves."

"Didn't Socrates believe that knowledge or wisdom would result in less unethical conduct?" asked Johnny.

"Yes, he did," I responded. "He saw intellectual and moral virtue as the same" (Plato, *Meno*).

"But that's not correct, is it?" asked Johnny. "It assumes that if someone *knows* what is good, he or she will *do* what is good."

Maria added, "Yes, that claim is refuted by the evidence of corruption we see everywhere in which people in positions of trust usually *know* what is proper and legal, yet they fail to do it."

"This makes ignorance the more fundamental problem of the two. Aristotle modified Socrates' view, holding that intellectual virtue and moral virtue are different and distinct," I replied. (Aristotle, *Nicomachean Ethics*)

"That helps to explain corruption and white-collar crime in general," Kelsey observed, "which is committed by people who know it is wrong, yet do it anyway."

"Overcoming ignorance with knowledge is an important first step, but it does not guarantee ethical conduct," I noted. "Something more is needed."

"And according to Aristotle, that would be moral virtue," Maria remarked.

"Indeed!" I said. "So there are two problems to be overcome in achieving a higher standard of ethical conduct. First, knowledge of what is ethical. Second, developing the moral virtue to act on that knowledge."

* * * * * * *

Virtue Ethics

"How difficult can these ethical principles be?" asked Johnny, eager for the semester to end.

"Would you prefer to be an ethical person, or do ethical acts?" I asked, ignoring his question.

"Aren't they the same thing?" said Kelsey.

I replied, "No. If you can achieve an ethical disposition, we can count on you to choose ethical conduct most of the time. If we look only at individual decisions, however..."

"Then you are only as good as your last decision," Maria completed the thought.

"It's like judging star athletes only on the strength of their last game," added Johnny.

"Precisely," I said. "And it's always wrong to judge people based on single decisions or actions, rather than on their character, as revealed by their history of action."

Maria went on, "Unlike his predecessors Socrates and Plato, Aristotle realized that intellectual virtue and moral virtue were very different things, and he developed a better ethical approach."

I added, "Intellectual virtue is important on its own, in order counter ignorance."

And didn't Aristotle say, 'it is in [our] power not to be ignorant'?" asked Maria.

"But that isn't enough to make you morally virtuous," I replied.

"What is moral virtue?" Kelsey asked the group.

"It's the disposition to make right (ethical) choices," replied Maria.

"How do we know when a choice is ethical?" continued Kelsey.

I inserted, "It comes down to two things: real goods and the moral virtues. Many human activities are aimed at *some* good, but some goods have more value than others do. You can work hard to enrich yourself, or choose to work hard to feed the poor. We can all agree that working hard is a good thing, but we would also agree that a goal of self-enrichment is not as good as working to feed the poor.

Aristotle thought a lot about this in conversations with his students, and came to realize that real goods are things we ought to desire, whether or not we really do."

Maria clarified, "The real goods are of three types:
1. bodily goods (food, shelter, health),
2. livelihood (wealth above the subsistence level, pleasure, knowledge),
3. social goods (liberty, friends/loved ones, and civil

peace)."

"So there are only nine real goods that everyone should desire?" asked Kelsey.

"That's about it," replied Johnny.

"Except that the ultimate good in life is happiness, which Aristotle argues is the final goal in pursuing the real goods over the course of your life," I added.

"What about chocolate?" said Kelsey.

"Other goods are apparent goods, some of which are innocuous and some are noxious. Chocolate is an innocuous apparent good, unless you overindulge and it interferes with your health (a real good)," said Maria.

"Yes," I agreed. "Apparent goods are O.K. only if they are done in moderation and do not interfere with the real goods."

"How much wealth is enough?" asked Kelsey.

I replied, "Wealth is needed only to live decently above the subsistence level. In fact, the three apparent goods most often pursued noxiously are wealth, fame, and power. The need for wealth is limited, and fame and power are not needed at all, yet pursuit of these three apparent goods lie at the root of most unethical and corrupt behavior we see."

"Ethical conduct sounds easy, so far," said Johnny,

"The problem comes for most of us in the way we pursue the real goods," added Maria.

I added, "Even though there's a lot of consensus about the real goods in life, many people lie, cheat, or steal to get them."

"What is moral virtue?" said Kelsey.

"It is excellence of character," I said.

"How do I become morally excellent?" asked Johnny.

Maria jumped in, "Aristotle identified 10 moral virtues: courage, temperance, prudence, justice, pride, ambition, having a good temper, being a good friend, truthfulness, and wittiness."

Kelsey asked, "These are the 10 traits that people are morally obligated to follow as they pursue the real goods?"

"Yes, that is the heart of virtue ethics---designed to create ethical people who will act ethically, by pursuing real goods, while following the moral virtues," I concluded.

Maria noted, "The moral virtues are a bit more difficult than they seem because they must be followed according to the 'mean' or middle, rather than to the extreme. For example, courage is a moral virtue, but to excess it becomes rashness, and too little courage is cowardice. Similarly, temperance is another virtue, but to excess is inhibition or self-denial, while too little temperance becomes self-indulgence."

"And a prudent person is not extravagant, but also not so careful as to lead to inaction," I added.

Maria went on, "Ambition is another moral virtue, but it falls on the mean between blind ambition at the expense of others on one hand, and laziness on the other."

"You get the idea," I said. "Even Aristotle admitted it was not easy. He said, 'It is no easy task to be good…to find the middle…anyone can get angry—that is easy—or give or spend money; but to do this to the right person, to the right extent, at the right time, with the right motive, and the right way, that is not for everyone, nor is it easy; wherefore goodness is both rare and laudable and noble.'" (*Nicomachean Ethics*, p. 45).

"I love that line: 'goodness is both rare and laudable and noble.'" said Kelsey.

"But in the end," Maria observed, "Aristotle declared, 'We are the masters of our actions from the beginning to the end.'"

"Aristotle does not offer a formula for being ethical in specific situations!" said Johnny in frustration. "He gives us the real goods to seek and the moral virtues to guide the journey, but individuals *must find their own way* in applying these principles in the situations they encounter."

I concluded, "There is no formula to guide your conduct in every circumstance that will arise during the course of your life, but pursuing real goods in accord with the moral virtues provides the ethical principles to guide your path."

* * * * *

Formalism

"What about other ethical perspectives, such as utilitarianism and formalism? Are they better?" asked Johnny.

I reported, "There are three major ethical perspectives that have endured over the centuries: virtue ethics, formalism, and utilitarianism. As we just saw, virtue ethics does not believe it is possible for an ethical 'formula' to solve every situation that arises. However, formalism and utilitarianism attempt to do just that."

Maria recognized, "Formalism was developed by Immanuel Kant during the 1700s. He argued that the morality of any action you take is determined by whether or not it violates a basic moral principle (rather than on any particular outcome that results). *If the principle is correct*, the act is ethical, according to this view. Formalism focuses on moral duty as set forth in just two basic principles." (Kant, *Grounding for the Metaphysics of Morals*).

"Yes, the two controlling moral principles for formalism are the categorical imperative and the practical imperative," I noted. "The categorical imperative states that you should never act in a way that the rule behind it shouldn't become a universal principle. The rule behind any action you take must be *universalizable*."

"I don't want to pay taxes because the government wastes my tax dollars on things I don't believe in," said Johnny.

"That's a bad universal rule, so it cannot be defended on ethical grounds," replied Maria.

"Why?"

"You don't have kids and might not want to pay school taxes, Kelsey might be a pacifist and does not want to support an army, and some people don't drive and don't want to spend money on highways. Taxes are for public goods, so we elect people to represent public desires in prioritizing public spending and the taxes needed to support them," concluded Maria.

"And if I don't like how that tax money is being spent?" asked Johnny.

"You elect different representatives!" I inserted. "That's the beauty of a representative democracy."

"Kant seems to make lying immoral," said Johnny.

"Yes," replied Maria. "It is a bad universal rule to lie, so lying is always unethical, because you should never make promises or statements you do not intend to keep, or believe to be true."

"Kant believed that lying. If you lie sometimes, how do I know when to believe you? Can you be expected to tell the truth only when it is convenient for you, or if it's what you think I want to hear?" asked Kelsey.

"Kant determined that 'truth is not a possession, the right to which can be granted to one person but refused to another…it is an unconditional duty which holds in all circumstances.'" I added. (*Grounding for the Metaphysics of Morals*, pp. 65–6).

"The second major part of formalism is the practical imperative," I continued, "which states that an ethical person never treats another person as a means to an end."

"What if I kill someone who is threatening the life of someone else?" asked Johnny.

"That is a commonly cited problem with formalism," I replied. "Killing one person to defend another is *using* a person as a means to an end, and therefore violates the practical imperative and is unethical."

"This shows the problem of determining ethical action on a case-by-case basis," added Maria.

"At the same time, the categorical imperative has appeal in when expectations of conduct can be stated in precise terms," I asserted. "For example, an ethical business philosophy is

'Act in a way that you would want your employees to act if you were the employer,' *and* 'Employers should treat employees as they would want to be treated if they were the employees.'" (see Barry, 1998; Bok, 1999).

"In the same way, public officials should act in ways they would want their constituents to act if <u>they</u> were the public official," *and* "officials should treat citizens as they would want to be treated if <u>they</u> were the public official." Kelsey injected.

"Therefore, Kant's ethical principles have clear value in understanding the proper ethical relationships between the powerful and those without such power," I concluded.

"So it appears that virtue ethics is directed at developing a moral *person* through a pattern of moral conduct, whereas formalism seeks to develop moral *actions* regardless of where they lead," Maria recognized.

* * * * *

Utilitarianism

"The third influential ethical perspective is utilitarianism developed by John Stuart Mill during the 1800s. While Aristotle focuses on virtue, Kant on moral duty, Mill focuses on utility," I summarized.

"Utility?" asked Kelsey.

"It means that ethical actions are determined based on the good that results from the action," I replied.

"So morality is determined by the *consequences* it brings, compared to other alternative actions?" asked Johnny.

Maria offered, "Utilitarianism sees pleasure and freedom from pain as the desirable ends of all action, so your conduct should be designed to produce happiness and avoid pain." (Mill, *Utilitarianism*)

"So must we always seek the greatest total happiness?" asked Johnny.

"Yes, the *total* happiness is the goal of ethical conduct, not your *individual* happiness," replied Maria.

"Mill believes there are two causes to an unsatisfactory life: selfishness and lack of mental cultivation," I added. "*Selfishness* is caring for nobody but oneself, which leads to unhappiness, because that person lacks both public and private good will that contribute greatly to happiness."

"Whereas a person with a *cultivated mind*," Kelsey offered, "is interested in everything, such as nature, art, poetry, history, and the future."

"So a lack of mental cultivation leads to indifference to all these things, and ultimately to unhappiness, according to Mill," said Maria. "Selfishness and an uncultivated mind are primary factors that hinder the achievement of happiness in the utilitarian view."

"And the way that decisions are made is important," I continued. "Individual ethical decisions must weigh the consequences toward yourself and others impartially. Your motivation is not important; only the outcome is important in the utilitarian perspective on ethics."

"What if I help a struggling friend cheat on her law exam, so she can make it through law school?" asked Johnny.

"Is this ethical under utilitarianism?" I asked no one in particular.

"Sure, you help your friend cheat, she graduates, but then fails the bar licensing exam because of her incompetence in law school," said Maria.

"Or the cheating is discovered, and you and your friend are tossed from law school," said Kelsey.

"It is very easy to weigh the possible consequences in a self-serving way," I added. "This is one of many examples that reveal a major problem with using 'utility' as an ethical premise. Our ability to know the future (i.e., the actual consequences of an act) makes utilitarianism a difficult criterion for ethical decisions."

"Neither virtue ethics, nor formalism, see utilitarianism as a useful ethical perspective," observed Maria.

←—————————————————————————→

"In one instance, a newspaper reporter went to New York City's Chinatown and was taken to three secret showrooms where she bought counterfeit handbags. The counterfeit bags were placed inside a dark garbage bag to hide them. The reporter spent $195 on six 'name brand' but counterfeit purses, which would have cost $3,000 retail for the authentic bags," I recounted the story.

"The reporter noted in the article, which she later wrote about her purchases, that the counterfeit trade supports Asian mafias, steals intellectual property from legitimate manufacturers, avoids millions of dollars in taxes, and is manufactured without any controls over the use of child labor or banned chemical products."

"But the story didn't end there," observed Maria.

"No, it didn't," I replied. "The reporter concluded in her article that, even though police target the makers and sellers of counterfeits, 'Casual buyers are unlikely to be busted,' and she then proceeded to give tips about how to buy the highest-quality fake purses!"

"What?" exclaimed Johnny.

"There was outrage from readers about this article when it appeared," I responded, "because it condoned buying illegal merchandise and thereby supporting illegal business and organized crime activity."

One critic said later, "I don't shop for counterfeit goods

anymore. The quality is poor, and the feeling of having something fake is worse. I hadn't thought of the Asian mafia angle until I read it in some of the readers' comments" (Schumacher-Matos, 2008).

"In this case, both the original reporter and the critic justified their behavior on its potential outcomes: The reporter focused on the low cost and likelihood of apprehension, whereas the critic focused on product quality, owning fake merchandise, and helping the mafia," observed Maria.

"This is an example of utilitarian thinking," continued Kelsey. "Their opposite conclusions (to buy counterfeits or not) focused entirely on their assessment of future consequences."

Johnny noted, "Kant's formalism would assess the conduct differently, permitting only one ethical course of conduct. Using the categorical and practical imperatives, the buying of counterfeits is both a bad universal rule and uses others (specifically, legitimate manufacturers, businesses, child laborers, and the illicit sellers) as a means to your personal goal of obtaining inexpensive purses."

"Therefore, buying counterfeit property cannot be justified under formalism. The ethical principles of formalism (focusing on the categorical and practical imperatives) make the purchase of counterfeit goods unethical on its face," I concluded.

"The likelihood of being caught, the product quality, impact on organized crime, or how you might feel about it afterwards ---- Kant sees all of these considerations as irrelevant to making a moral decision because they are mere after-the-fact rationalizations," added Maria.

"Moral decisions must be made *a priori* under formalism, after considering both the categorical and practical imperatives, and ignoring any subsequent impact your conduct may or may not have," I added.

Kelsey took up the argument. "Virtue ethics would evaluate the situation differently by asking what real goods are being pursued with the purchase of counterfeit goods? The answer is none, so the ethical decision is easy. The purchase of counterfeit goods also violates several of the moral virtues, such as temperance, prudence, justice, and truthfulness."

"So virtue ethics answers the question of what an ethical *person* would do, whereas formalism and utilitarianism focus on the circumstances of the particular *act* in question," Johnny noted.

"Yes," I replied. "Formalism requires moral duty according to a couple of universal principles where individual motivation is paramount. Virtue ethics see the principle of utility as a means-end maxim of expediency, but not reflective of moral virtue. Virtue ethics does not see the need for rules of conduct for all acts and situations as set forth by formalism or utilitarianism, because pursuing real goods while following the moral virtues, offers all the guidance an ethical person needs."

Maria added, "Working toward developing ethical *people*, as envisioned by Aristotle, is more likely to produce ethical decisions than the act-based and case-based approaches of the other ethical perspectives."

"The ethical values encompassed by the real goods and moral virtues offer principles for standards and guidance for ethical conduct. It is against these standards that our actions and choices can be evaluated," I concurred.

It has been said, "corruption is often the end of a slippery slope consisting of small misjudgments and gradual acceptance" of unethical conduct, Kelsey recalled. (OECD, 2018:43).

"A summary of the three major ethical perspectives shows the differences in the goals of ethical behavior, the means of becoming ethical, and how ethical conduct is to be judged according to virtue ethics, formalism, and utilitarianism.

Summarizing Three Ethical Perspectives

	Virtue Ethics	**Formalism**	**Utilitarianism**
Goals of ethical behavior	A life that is most desirable results in ethical happiness, achieved by pursuing real goods through virtuous action.	Do moral duty.	Seek the greatest total happiness.
Means of being ethical	Follow the moral virtues: "By doing just acts…the just person is produced."	The categorical imperative is the supreme principle of morality.	Maximize pleasure while minimizing pain.

	Virtue Ethics	**Formalism**	**Utilitarianism**
Judging ethical conduct	Good conduct cannot be prescribed. Individual acts can be misleading unless they come from "a firm and unchangeable character." Virtue is a mean or middle that aims at the intermediate and avoids excess and defect.	Assess all actions according to categorical and practical imperatives. Consequences of acts do not bear on moral decisions, because other causes can result in the outcome. Personal inclinations have no moral value.	Make individual decisions by weighing the consequences toward yourself and toward others equally and impartially. Individual motivation is not relevant; only the outcome matters.

All the ethical theories are internally consistent in the way they determine the goals, means, and criteria for judging conduct (the 'what'), but there are large differences in the purpose or goal of ethical conduct (the 'why')." I argued.

"These distinctions can make the evaluation of ethical conduct difficult," said Kelsey.

"But not impossible," added Maria. "When conduct is evaluated using these perspectives, it becomes easy to see the ethical path by making the logical connections among means, goals, and the ways that ethical conduct is judged."

Johnny concluded, "We now have a general idea of the principles of ethical decision-making. How do we make this work in practice?"

* * * * * * * *

CHAPTER 2

Developing Good Habits:
Learning how to apply principles in practice

"I believe that people have a 'moral compass' that guides them in making decisions," said Johnny.

"Oh, you mean like Hitler, Mussolini, Idi Amin, and the rest of them?" replied Maria accusingly.

"OK, their moral compass was warped, but they had reasons for what they did," said Johnny.

"But they were not ethical reasons," inserted Maria.

"So where does the moral compass come from?" asked Kelsey.

Knowing What Ethical Principles Are

"Yes, Johnny, people often claim the existence of an internal moral compass, but few have any idea what that is. It is often a cloak to cover self-serving or selfish instincts," noted Maria.

"But the average person cares about others, often due to proper upbringing which emphasizes to them as children to be considerate of others," replied Johnny. (Aquino and Reed,

2002).

"But this doesn't translate into ethical behavior without an understanding of what ethical principles are," I observed.

Maria added, "Yes, it's more than caring about others. People tend to make selfish choices; looking out for personal advantage is hard-wired into the human psyche. Let's face that fact. Most instances of rude, impatient, and even criminal behavior are the result of *selfish* choices---placing your own interests above that of others."

"So what's missing is the ability to recognize self-serving choices," I added. "This involves developing the skills needed to recognize ethical dilemmas through education, practice, and training in applying them in your life."

"Recognizing an ethical dilemma when it presents itself must come first," concluded Maria.

Critical Thinking

"Utilitarianism is a common justification for public policy decisions in which the rights of the many usually outweigh the rights of the few." I began the class. "But there are many exceptions that show fault in this type of thinking. What are they?"

"I have an example," replied Johnny. "Disabled persons will always be a distinct minority, so why should the government invest in wheelchair ramps, lower curbs, and other accommodations for them?"

"It is because the rights of the few matter in ethical terms," added Maria.

"Yes," I replied. "It is important that ethics is not turned into a mere cost-benefit calculation. That kind of thinking results in overlooking the valid claims of minorities. Ethical principles protect not only the rights of minorities, but the rights of every person and taxpayer who might be exploited by low visibility business or government decisions that misspend public money, or harm consumers, or the general public."

"We need to think critically about these issues, otherwise we risk trampling on the overlooked concerns of groups outside the majority," added Kelsey.

I continued. "Critical thinking has become the mantra of those looking to change the way education and learning occur. Rather than emphasizing the accumulation of facts, which dominates education today, critical thinking emphasizes instead the ability to evaluate viewpoints, facts, and behaviors objectively, in order to assess the presentation of information ---and methods of argumentation--- to establish the true worth of an act or course of conduct."

Maria chimed in, "Critical thinking is the basis for making decisions in situations where the facts are unclear or conflict."

"Or in cases where it is inconvenient to consider the rights of others," Johnny added, "because it will cost money and divert attention from the inexorable demands of the majority."

"How to make decisions is not routinely taught. That is to say, we never learn how to use facts in a principled way," added Maria.

"Critical thinking involves the development of abilities to sort through facts intelligently, as well as half-truths, lies, and deceptive arguments, in order to determine the actual value of a statement, position, or behavior," I concluded. (Facione, 1990).

Kelsey added a crucial point. "In essence, critical thinking is about discerning truth. Pursuing truth is the goal of all endeavors, including education."

"And the truth consists of beliefs that align with objective facts. Too often, we want to believe an idea or opinion that conforms to our pre-existing beliefs without making an effort to ascertain its *actual* truth." Maria declared.

"I agree," said Johnny. "Truth and falsity are determined by *facts*, and not the *beliefs* of people. Critical thinking provides the method to determine the truth by helping to separate deceptive use of information and arguments that mask false or misleading statements." (Shapiro, 2010; Visser-Wijnveen et al. 2009).

"But how can critical thinking be taught?" asked Maria.

"There is disagreement in the literature about how to accomplish this in practice," I replied. "Some believe critical thinking emphasizes the 'critical,' resulting in cynical disbelief, rather than looking for real meaning. Others point to examples of bad or absent critical thinking on the part of individuals and organizations, but the precise methods for inculcating this skill are elusive for many, especially for students."

"So what are the characteristics of a critical thinker?" asked Kelsey.

"A consensus document identified characteristics of the critical thinker: 'The ideal critical thinker is habitually inquisitive, well-informed, trustful of reason, open-minded, flexible, fair-minded in evaluation, honest in facing personal biases, prudent in making judgments, willing to reconsider, clear about issues, orderly in complex matters, diligent in seeking relevant information, reasonable in the selection of criteria, focused in inquiry, and persistent in seeking results which are as precise as the subject and the circumstances of inquiry permit'" (Roth, 2010).

"These are all desirable characteristics," Johnny agreed, "but how do we work toward these goals, while we're taking courses on a variety of different substantive topics?"

"This situation led me to create a one-page series of questions for students to use to become more critical in how they think," I replied. "It is titled, *A Method to Evaluate Viewpoints and to Think Critically: How not to be fooled or misled by weak arguments*, and it designed to offer a concise way to operationalize the meaning of critical thinking."

A Method to Evaluate Viewpoints and to Think Critically
How not to be fooled or misled by weak arguments

A. Author's Background
  1. Is the author qualified to speak on the topic?
  2. Is his/her background likely to affect the views expressed?

B. Principal Contention (PC): What is the main point(s) the author is making?
C. Supporting Evidence: What are the arguments used by the author to sustain his or her principal contention?
D. How Confident or Wary Should We Be About This Viewpoint? (i.e., *ways to think critically*).

  1. *Recognizing Deceptive Information*

a. **Disputable Information Source**: Is the source of information valid and reliable? (i.e., are data or valid scientific studies employed versus personal experiences and anecdotes)?
b. **Factual Errors**: Do you possess knowledge that refutes the author's argument? What is its source? Is it reliable information?
c. **Ideological Statements**: Can the arguments made be evaluated by some kind of objective evidence, or is it unprovable?
d. **Unsupported Assertion**: Are the supporting arguments based on reliable facts and evidence or only opinions?
e. **Unwarranted Generalization**: Are facts or statistics used about one case to generalize unjustly about an entire group?

  2. *Recognizing Deceptive Methods of Argumentation*

a. **Bad Logic**: Is there a reasonable connection, or causal relation, between the evidence used and the principal contention?
b. **Categorical Statement**: Is the argument made in such a way that it appears there can be no other logical alternative?
c. **Conjecture**: Are inferences or predictions made based on incomplete information or guesswork?
d. **Exaggeration**: Is an opposing point of view distorted or misrepresented to make the author's own view appear stronger?
e. **Imitation**: Is an assumption made that "everybody" does or should believe in a particular point of view?
f. **Inflammatory Language**: Is an attempt made to persuade using hysterical or emotionally charged language instead of reason?
g. **Intimidation**: Is there an implied threat that if you don't do or believe something, you are in serious trouble?

> h. **Personal Attack**: Is an opponent criticized personally, rather than a rational debate of his or her ideas?
> i. **Sensationalism**: Is the argument made in a manner that is intended to shock or titillate, rather than inform?
> j. **Testimonial**: Do others quoted to support the author's views have expertise in the area?

"Does this work?" asked Maria.

"I provide students with editorials, commentary, and blogs that express a point of view, and have them apply this 'Method' to assess whether or not the arguments and conclusions should be believed. I have had some success with this approach," I replied.

"I suppose it helps people distinguish strong arguments from weak ones," observed Kelsey.

"And that is the essence of critical thinking," I replied.

Decisions in the public v. private interest

"I was in line at the grocery store check-out one day, and the person in front of me was frustrated. She said, 'You mean all you have is a check to pay for this?!' to an elderly woman who was paying the cashier with a check and taking a few minutes to write it."

"Do you have any thoughts on this kind of behavior by the frustrated woman?" I asked.

"It is poor etiquette," said Kelsey.

"But is it unethical?" asked Johnny.

"We must remember that ethics is the study of morality, and

that morals are good conduct, constituting permissible behavior." I reminded the group.

"So unethical behavior is really another way to say immoral behavior?" asked Kelsey.

"Yes, but we often use the term 'morality' as conduct we prefer, when it is actually conduct that is ethically wrong," added Maria.

"That seems to be the important difference, then," waxed Johnny. "In both cases, we are talking about human behavior that has moral content."

"Behavior that does not affect others does not have moral content," I added.

"Although I can't think of an example," said Kelsey.

"Neither can I," added Maria. "I imagine there are very few examples of actions that lack moral content because most everything we do has impacts on other people."

"So the vast majority of all our behavior has moral content because it affects others, and therefore the principles of ethics apply to it," Johnny concluded.

"The acts of public officials, who by definition represent the public interest in their actions, have even greater ethical consequence," I transitioned the conversation.

"Consider the case of The Dove Spa, a massage parlor in the Midwest. A plainclothes undercover detective entered, and asked for the services of one of the women working there.

The woman didn't know was that the man was a police officer, wearing a hidden recording device. In exchange for $100 plus a $35 tip, she fondled the officer's genitals."

"And what's the problem with that?" asked Johnny.

"The officer went back four additional times, according to an affidavit released later. During that time, spanning five months, the officer also visited a massage parlor in another town, and each time, he allowed the women---all Asian immigrants---to fondle him in exchange for cash, in a purported effort against prostitution and human trafficking."

"This sounds like a problem." Johnny recognized.

"The police department defended their methods after 30 officers raided two businesses, arrested six people, including four alleged prostitutes and two alleged pimps. But the methods were criticized by legal and law enforcement experts and women's advocates as excessive, unnecessary, and misapplied to an investigation that involved possible human trafficking." (Borgman, 1995; Goldstein, 2013; Sabalow, 2013).

"Is this morally permissible conduct?" I asked the group. "Remember, it is important first to recognize the ethical issue here."

"Is it morally permissible for a police officer to engage in sex acts in order to make a prostitution case against a massage parlor?" stated Johnny.

"Yes, that's the central issue of moral permissibility here," I replied.

"It's absolutely <u>not</u> permissible!" replied Maria. "What went on during the visits was unnecessary, and a large number of visits also casts doubt on the law enforcement officer's true motives."

"This is a 'right versus right' dilemma in which two principles conflict. Therefore, a way to determine which principle is more important is needed in this scenario." (Kidder, 1996).

"There are some relevant and specific issues, which bear on this issue," added Kelsey. "Were 5 visits necessary, or were they exploitive or selfish or excessive?"

"Were there other ways for the police to produce the evidence of prostitution, such as relying on accounts from subsequently arrested or detained customers, or responding to complaints?" added Maria.

"Aristotle might put it this way," I continued. "Were police seeking a real good in accord with the moral virtues—such as balancing temperance versus self-indulgence, prudence versus hedonism, or pursuing real versus apparent goods?"

"In distinguishing integrity of public officials from the integrity of private individuals, it is important to realize that public integrity exists to the extent the decisions of public officials correspond to the *public* interest," I argued.

"Likewise," added Johnny, "the decisions of private individuals should account for not only their own ethical nature but also the interests of others around them. Therefore, there is an inherent social component of ethical thought."

"Virtually all of our conduct affects others, therefore we must be thoughtful and ethical in all our actions," Maria summarized the issue.

Legal, but unethical and Denial of Harm

Two Tennessee brothers, ages 21 and 36, came up with an idea during the COVID-19 pandemic, when hand sanitizer and antibacterial wipes were scarce. The brothers canvassed dollar stores and other retailers across Tennessee and Kentucky, and bought large quantities of hand sanitizer and antibacterial wipes during the early stages of the coronavirus pandemic.

They sold 300 bottles of hand sanitizer on Amazon for $8 to $70 each, earning a steep profit. The next day, Amazon pulled their items from Amazon.com, along with those of thousands of other sellers like them.

The result was the brothers had stockpiled nearly 18,000 bottles of hand sanitizer, but now had no way to sell them. "Was the conduct of the Tennessee brothers morally permissible?"

"I know it's illegal in some states for businesses to charge 'unreasonable' prices for essential goods or services during a disaster," said Johnny.

"But it's not illegal in most places," added Maria. "And why do you think those laws were enacted?"

"Because people did it!" exclaimed Kelsey.

"There is widespread preoccupation with our personal happiness and success, rather than concern for others. Because our actions virtually always impact others, we should have their interests at the center of our vision." I emphasized.

"I heard that the brothers received hate mail and death threats once their scam became known," Johnny offered.

"The brothers' conduct is clearly unethical under any ethical perspective," said Kelsey. "It violates several of Aristotle's moral virtues, Kant's categorical imperative, and Mill's total happiness."

"If this conduct is universally unethical, why did the brothers do it?" I asked the group.

"They probably denied they were doing any harm to the victims, even though it is clear they helped create a shortage and then overcharged the customers in need," replied Kelsey.

"I am happy to report that Aristotle's concept of justice did ensue in the case," I noted. "Under the settlement terms in this case, the brothers agreed to donate all their accumulated supplies to their church for distribution to local emergency responders, but they are not able to recoup the thousands of dollars they spent on the sanitary supplies" (Vigdor, 2020).

"It's an example of conduct that is unethical, but yet legal in most places," added Maria. "The law does not appear to capture a lot of objectionable conduct."

Johnny responded, "The law provides only the baseline or outer boundaries of acceptable civil behavior."

"Moral behavior requires more than the law requires," I concluded.

CHAPTER 3

Forgetting Who You Are:
Moral Reminders

"It's important not to forget that we overrate ourselves when it comes to acting ethically," I began the class, which was meeting outside, although too near a mobile coffee wagon on campus.

"Are you calling us unethical?" replied Johnny defensively.

"Let's leave it that you are less consistently ethical than you think," said Kelsey, sitting down with a large, iced, double espresso with foamed milk topped with whipped cream and sprinkles for some reason.

"What is that drink?" said Johnny.

"Heaven on earth!" Kelsey responded.

"You mean you can find heaven on a campus coffee wagon?" asked Maria with some surprise.

"You have to be looking for it," replied Kelsey.

Moral culture

"I believe the issue at hand is overrating our own ethical standing." I re-inserted myself into the conversation.

"And how do you know we over-rate our own ethics?" asked Johnny.

"It's up to each of us to establish our personal moral culture in which we make responsible and ethically principled decisions in our everyday lives," I replied. "We are accountable for developing a professional moral culture in which our professional decisions are similarly principled and ethical."

"I think he's got a case study coming for us," said Maria to the other students.

"There is lots of experimental evidence, as well as examples from real life, that reveal our true leanings," I continued. "There was the case in New York of a guy named Ben, who went to his bank to withdraw some cash, and the bank teller told him, to his great surprise, his account balance was 5 million dollars! Ben tried to correct the mistake, but the bank teller insisted that was his balance. So what do you think Ben did?"

"He went to the bank manager to correct the error?" exclaimed Maria.

"No, he took the money," Johnny surmised.

"I'm afraid he withdrew a total of $2 million, a few thousand dollars at a time, over a period of five weeks. His idea was that he would invest the money in the stock market, earn money on his investments, and then return the original $2 million to the bank account." I recounted.

"His ship came in!" said Johnny excitedly.

"There was no ship, and it didn't come in." I reminded him. "Can you guess what happened next?"

"His investments did not go well, and he lost the money," replied Kelsey. "The money actually belonged to a man with the same name, and the bank credited the funds to the wrong man named Ben."

"That's right," I noted.

"So what happened?" asked Johnny.

"Ben was charged with grand larceny, when it was discovered that he withdrew and spent a chunk of the money during his five-week investing spree," replied Kelsey.

"Why were Ben's actions clearly unethical conduct?" I asked.

"Because they were against the law?" asked Maria.

"No, they would have been unethical, even without the law," replied Kelsey. "He appropriated something that did not belong to him, and he knew it all along."

Self-serving bias

"His scheme was also self-serving, lacking regard for the money's true owner and the possibility of losing it," I added.

"An interesting comment was offered by Ben's mother, who said, 'I don't know what happened. He's always been a good son to me. He's never been in trouble with the law.'"

"Ben's wife, Maxine, added, 'He's a good guy, he's a family man.'"

"And what does *that* have to do with it?" said Johnny.

"Exactly!" I added. "Both Ben and his family suffered from what is called a self-serving bias. This occurs when we *believe* our actions are both objective and ethical, when *in fact* they are actually neither."

"As I recall," said Maria, "this is something that John Stuart Mill was quite concerned about in making ethical judgments. He said the consequences of your conduct toward yourself and others must be weighed equally and impartially."

"This is difficult to do, however, because *you* are the one who figures to gain or lose from the decision!" Kelsey replied.

I emphasized, "It is important to remember that self-serving bias is common, and an ethical person must always be alert to defining any situation in ways that do not overstate their own personal benefit or minimize the valid interests of others."

Self-serving bias occurs in the professions as well.

"Investigations by detectives can be influenced by pressure from the public, the media, or prosecutors to crack a notorious case quickly. That pressure often pushes detectives to rely on evidence that corroborates their assumptions or hunches" (Handelman, 2019; Hill, Memon, & McGeorge, 2008).

"This is called 'confirmation bias,' when seizing upon facts that confirm your pre-existing hunches. The problem is that it is not objective thinking, and it obstructs the search for evidence that might lead in another direction." I noted.

"So a good detective should look just as hard for evidence that would exonerate a suspect, as he or she does in looking for evidence of guilt?" asked Johnny.

Maria replied, "A serious, broader look at *all* the evidence is the only way to guard against self-serving confirmation bias that results in unethical (and incorrect) decisions."

Counter Justifications

"I never committed any unethical behavior without a good justification for it!" Johnny shouted.

"And what's the problem with that statement?" I asked the group.

Maria responded, "It's using some random excuse you come up with to violate an ethical principle."

"There are many examples of employees 'borrowing' company funds or property without permission because they say they intend to pay it back," added Kelsey.

"Or denying that any serious harm was caused by your action," added Maria.

"These are self-serving justifications used to reconcile your unethical conduct --- in an effort to convince yourself that it's not really unethical," I concluded the thought.

"So it's a vain effort to redefine what you're doing as not serious, inconsequential, that everyone else does it, or that it's not actually wrong?" asked Johnny.

Maria replied, "It is a way to try to convince yourself you are acting ethically when you are not. It is a justification, or counter justification, which fools no one."

"Like in all education, nothing lasts forever. Studies of university graduates universities find that after only a few years, former students forget basic facts they had learned," I noted. (Rubin, 2014; Students, 2007).

Kelsey added, "The same is true for ethics. People do not forget about ethics, but they forget that ethical principles exist and apply in all situations, leaving room for excuses and rationalizations ranging from 'changing times' to 'extenuating circumstances.'"

"Sounds like weak justifications to me," said Maria.

"I agree," said Kelsey. "That's because they are unethical, and do not survive scrutiny when applying ethical principles."

Nudges

"How do we establish a moral culture that does not become self-serving?" asked Johnny.

"One way to counter self-serving biases and justification is through 'nudges' that help to push us toward making ethical choices." I replied.

"What's a nudge?" asked Kelsey.

"Nudges are methods to get you to consider ethical choices

more clearly and more often," replied Maria. "Reminders about ethical conduct, like reporting business gifts, or ethics surveys and periodic training that is convenient and engaging, helps put ethical thought back toward the top of people's thinking." (see Thaler & Sunstein, 2009).

"Before it slides back down once again," added Johnny.

"Yes, that's true for many people," noted Maria.

"Studies have found that reminding individuals through periodic training and reinforcement of expected behaviors, and reminders about unacceptable conduct, are useful tools in promoting, reminding, and encouraging ethical conduct," I added. (Bursztyn et al., 2015; Pruckner & Sausgruber, 2013).

"I read a study that found that vote-buying in the Philippines was reduced, after people were asked to make a promise not to sell their vote in the forthcoming election," observed Kelsey. (Hicken et al., 2015).

"In India, an NGO created a zero rupee note that looked like real currency, but has a '0' on it with a statement: 'I promise to neither accept or give a bribe'" (5th Pillar, 2020; World Bank, 2015). These notes have been widely distributed to reinforce the public will against corruption," said Maria.

"There are instances, small and large, of moral reminders making a significant difference in the ethical behavior of individuals around the world," I observed.

"You had us read a favorite study of mine," said Johnny. "An experiment was designed to reduce the number of newspapers being taken from newspaper vending machines (which permit a person to purchase a single paper, but also take additional copies without payment). They added a sign to the machine, 'Thank you for being honest.' The sign made a noticeable difference in the number of papers stolen without payment!"

"There are similar studies of moral reminders about honesty to college students prior to taking exams, which have had similar results," I added. "Moral reminders appear to have at least short-term effects." (Grym & Liljander, 2016; Isakov & Tripathy, 2017).

"Unlike in the US, public officials in many countries are not permitted to accept gifts due to the conflict of interest (public versus private) such conduct creates," said Kelsey.

"In Mexico, messages are sent to officials near the end of the year, reminding them that any gifts must be reported, and this increases self-reporting of gifts," reported Maria. "The interesting part was that this *positive* reminder of legal obligations has a stronger impact than did reminders about the *penalties* for misconduct." (OECD, 2018).

"There is also other empirical evidence that shows that moral reminders focused on rewarding honesty produce ethical behavior more often than do threats of penalties for misconduct," I added. (Fellner, Sausgruber, & Traxler, 2013; Pruckner & Sausgruber, 2013).

"Of course, the reason for the difference in effect is the certainty," argued Johnny. "Threats of sanctions apply only to those caught, and people generally believe (correctly) that the odds of apprehension are low. Therefore, appealing to ethical beliefs and training is more compelling to the person reading the appeal to their honesty."

"And it shows that moral nudges help to push people back toward the ethical path," Maria observed.

"I guess we all need some positive reinforcement in our lives," added Kelsey.

"To remind us of how we ought to behave," clarified Johnny.

"And it appears to work," I concluded.

CHAPTER 4

Responding to Violations: Accountability for Conduct

You are familiar with the case of George Floyd, a 46-year-old black man, who was killed in Minneapolis, Minnesota, in 2020 during an arrest for allegedly passing a counterfeit bill. During the arrest, a white police officer knelt on Floyd's neck for almost 9 minutes, while Floyd was handcuffed and lying face down, repeatedly saying "I can't breathe."

"That is clearly unethical and illegal because there was no reason for the prolonged choking of Floyd when he was down and handcuffed," observed Maria.

"Videos taken of the event by witnesses and security cameras documented this incident of death by extended strangulation, followed by two autopsies, which confirmed Floyd's death as a homicide, and the officer was charged with murder," I reported. "The entire world was able to see this event on video, and Floyd's death resulted in demonstrations and protests in more than 2,000 U.S. cities and also in many other places around the world---focusing on police brutality, racism, and lack of police accountability in multiple deaths involving black suspects in police custody."

"This is not a difficult ethical situation," concluded Johnny, "because it is disregarding the life of another, and also violating the rules of self-defense, or defense of others. So the principal officer involved is both legally and ethically wrong."

"The memorable part of this incident from an ethical viewpoint is the conduct of the other officers at the scene," I observed. "Two other police officers helped in restraining Floyd, and a third officer kept bystanders from intervening, who were pleading for the first officer to remove his knee from Floyd's neck."

"Why did the other officers fail to intervene, when it was clear that Floyd was subdued, on the ground, in handcuffs, and posed no threat?" asked Kelsey. "Why didn't any of them intervene to end the unnecessary killing of Floyd over a period of more than 8 minutes?"

"Difficult to say," replied Maria. "They were afraid of a more senior officer? Afraid of violating the chain of command? Afraid to contradict the actions of another officer?"

"You are probably correct," I replied. "But what do any of those rationalizations have to do with ethical conduct?"

"Nothing," said Johnny.

Maria continued, "The other officers clearly had a moral (and legal) obligation to act, but they did not. That is the ethical tragedy that occurred in this situation, in addition to the human tragedy."

"Someone was being killed in slow-motion over 8 minutes, and people with an ability to stop it did nothing," Kelsey said with astonishment.

"So we have an outrageous act of homicide occurring over a prolonged period of time, but trained police officers with an ability to intervene did not," I concluded. "This shows they either did not understand what their ethical obligation was, or they lacked the courage to act on it."

"I remember that courage is one of the moral virtues," said Kelsey.

"It's difficult to underestimate the importance of the courage to act ethically," I replied. "The Floyd incident is one of thousands throughout history, where evil was occurring, yet there was a failure of others to act with ethical courage."

Maria responded, "I remember reading about those who worked for Hitler during World War II, and cases of police or military officers, and government workers, who silently or actively supported corrupt conduct, acting as apologists for political dictators and authoritarian leaders at the local and national levels."

"Misplaced loyalty inhibits the reporting of unethical conduct or whistle-blowing on governmental misconduct," I noted.

Johnny claimed, "Loyalty is often a good attribute, but it is not a virtue in itself. When it is treated as a virtue, loyalty can be misguided, leading to protection of illicit conduct of all kinds in the name of 'loyalty.'"

Kelsey chimed in, "I saw where the U.S. Naval Academy includes as part of its educational program a visit to the Holocaust Museum in Washington, D.C. to show the sailors the extreme consequences of misplaced loyalty, blind obedience, and lack of compassion."

"Altruism is derived from the Latin *alter*, which means 'other.' Altruistic behavior is conduct undertaken in the interest or for the good of others; the opposite of self-centered desire," I remarked.

"That is the antidote for misguided loyalty---a knowledge that truth is a moral virtue, whereas loyalty is not," stressed Maria.

Johnny continued the thought, "As soon as loyalty ignores or plunders the truth, it becomes unethical conduct, which invariably victimizes others."

"A research study on altruism asked the question, 'Why did ordinary people risk their lives to protect Jews hiding from the Nazis during World War II?' In interviews with Holocaust survivors, the author found that heroes develop over time, taking early steps toward altruistic behavior, and then they begin to see themselves differently" (Staub, 2003; Kahana et al., 1985).

"This suggests that ethical conduct probably proceeds in the same way: from smaller acts to more consistent courses of conduct," Maria summarized.

"There are lots of examples of exemplary ethical conduct, where people not only act in consideration of others, but they extend themselves or take risks to do it," I informed the group. "The Underground Railroad helped slaves escape from bondage, and many people today simply extend themselves to assist others in need, by giving of their time, treasure, or talent."

"On the other hand, a genocide occurred in Rwanda during the 1990s, in which 800,000 Tutsis (the minority) were slaughtered over a period of 100 days by Hutus (the majority) in an effort to exterminate them entirely. Individuals and governments around the world turned their heads from this situation, avoiding the use of the term genocide, and failing to intervene, thereby allowing it to occur," I reported. (Gourevitch, 1999; Ilibagiza, 2007).

"How is that possible?" asked Maria.

"Hopefully, lessons were learned from Rwanda, as a subsequent international adjudication was carried out to assess responsibility, and apologies for inaction were made by multiple countries from around the world," I noted. (Power, 2001; Raghavan, 2014).

"Looking at it from the other side, what makes people generous and helpful in responding to the needs of others, rather than ignoring them or remaining bystanders in life?" asked Kelsey.

"That is ethics in action!" replied Maria.

Transparency without Enforcement

It was late, must have been after 1:00 am. I was returning from having a few drinks after a reception, and now I'm approaching the turnstile to the subway.

As I'm fishing for my metro card, the thought occurs to me, "No one's around. Why don't I jump the turnstile without paying? What do you think was my very next thought?"

"You might get caught!" said Kelsey from the back of the class.

"Yes, that's the most common reaction people have!" I replied.

"Why not consider the fact that it's unethical (and illegal)!" added Maria from the front row.

"I get to that thought pretty quickly, and so do my students, but many people never get there," I observed.

"Because they never learned what's ethical and what's not?" asked Kelsey.

"Precisely."

"So a fear of apprehension is needed to reinforce ethical conduct?" asked Maria.

"Because most people do not know ethics, and those that do often don't think much about consequences," chimed in Johnny.

"So are you saying we're all utilitarians, making our ethical decisions based only on the probable consequences?" said Kelsey.

"I don't think so, because experience suggests that there are lots of situations where we act ethically, even though the odds of apprehension for unethical conduct are low," added Maria.

"How often do you stop in the supermarket to buy

groceries?" I asked.

"Too often!" replied Johnny.

"Weekly!" said Maria.

"Daily!" answered Kelsey.

"Most supermarkets are set up so you can freely walk through the displayed merchandise. What are the odds of being caught, if you picked up an item and put it in your pocket?" I asked.

"The odds of apprehension are very low," countered Johnny.

"So why don't you steal from the supermarket regularly?" I pursued the questioning.

"Because it's unethical?" inquired Maria.

"Yes, we're making progress! In the case of supermarkets, it is not the odds of apprehension that keep you from stealing, because the odds are quite low," I continued.

"This suggests that utilitarianism has limits in that the consequences do not appear to be a major factor in supermarket theft," Johnny observed.

"If the odds of apprehension were the important factor in supermarket shoplifting decisions, the shelves should be bare! Everything should be stolen!" thought Maria aloud.

"There are certain stores and neighborhoods where theft is more common, and I see more surveillance cameras," remarked Johnny.

"And keep in mind that those cameras are watching store employees as much as they are customers," I added.

"So it's not entirely aimed at preventing theft by customers?" asked Kelsey.

"Nope. Employee theft is a larger threat than customer theft for many businesses." I replied.

"So what would happen if thefts from these stores became much more common?" asked Kelsey.

"Legislators would probably increase the penalties for theft!" Johnny mused. "But that would have no effect because it misunderstands their motivation. They are not stealing because the penalties are low."

"Correct! They are stealing because they do not appreciate the wrongfulness of the conduct and the impact it has on the victim." I observed.

"Or the impact on themselves as human beings," added Maria.

"Ethics education focuses attention on correcting this kind of self-centered thinking," I remarked. "Ethics and integrity policies and practices in companies, and the civil and criminal law itself, assume that people weigh the potential consequences of their actions."

"You mean the likelihood of being caught?" asked Kelsey.

"Yes, but this assumes a high level of monitoring and enforcement," Johnny thought aloud.

"Realistically, many decisions occur in low visibility situations," Maria considered, "especially unethical decisions which, nearly always, you do not want others to know about!"

"Threats of monitoring and surveillance are insufficient to produce deterrence. An empty police car at the side of the road will deter speeders. However, if multiple police cars are empty, the deterrent effect soon dissipates." I observed.

"I read where transparency that is not observed by others 'can be compared to a security camera without anyone to watch the tapes.'" Johnny remarked. (OECD, 2018, p. 23).

"Of course, ethical misconduct can be brazen. In the modern world, there have been cases of business leaders and government officials who say, 'I didn't hide what we were doing,' as if that was absolution for engaging in unethical conduct."

"When powerful interests involving the government or corporations exploit citizens, it is up to civil society and the media to point to the unethical conduct. The behavior may or may not be legal, but the purpose is to make clear that the conduct was not blameless and involved clear victims." Maria concluded.

"Like the common public corruption of appointing relatives or friends to government positions, or using public money for a personal advantage?" asked Kelsey.

"Civil society and the media must be able to voice concern in the face of misconduct, especially misconduct by the powerful. It's fundamental to maintaining the integrity of business and government in the eyes of the public," observed Maria.

"What is civil society?" Johnny asked.

"It's non-governmental organizations (NGOs), academia, private citizens, and the private sector," replied Maria.

"Civil society is the 'third sector' of society---outside of government and business," echoed Kelsey.

"Yes, transparency is important but equally important is unethical conduct being call out for what it is: thereby making rationalizations for that conduct more difficult to justify," I added.

Maria continued, "It seems that civil society and the media are the two groups to perform this public 'calling out' of questionable or unethical conduct, and conflicts of interest, because these acts are often carried out on behalf of the interests of governments or corporations, who either rationalize or attempt to conceal their unethical conduct."

Reducing distance

"I don't have to worry as much as others do about ethics, because I don't do important work," said Kelsey.

"Hold on," I replied. "It is easy to downgrade the significance of your actions. If you frame your conduct as not crucial to an ultimate outcome, you give yourself license to be mediocre and disregard your moral responsibility."

"It's actually a form of deception that you, or anyone, lacks a moral obligation to act ethically and responsibly," added Johnny. "Most of my friends are simply accepting and tolerant of others, but that doesn't seem like enough."

"The problem with tolerance is that it makes room for other people, but it does not produce an obligation to take any responsibility for them or their welfare," observed Maria. "There is no principle to guide your action if all you believe in is tolerance for others." (Messner, 2020).

"And some behaviors, like unethical conduct, should not be tolerated!" noted Kelsey.

"Every individual action a person takes (or fails to take) affects his or her ethical standing in some way," observed Maria.

"It can be argued that there is no such thing as a small ethical decision," I argued. "Take the example of a police recruit in class of the Georgia State Patrol trooper academy. One cadet, and it could have been you, knew that some of the 33 recruits in the class were struggling with the written exams at the academy, but the exams were easy for you. You were simply a better student, so you shared your notes and posted test questions and answers on a text messaging app. You didn't see it as a big deal, and it ingratiated you with the other recruits who are not doing as well at the academy."

"This is exactly what happened in Georgia. Of course, your 'small' unethical decision soon mushroomed. Two Snapchat group chats were also created that included members of the class."

"And then the rumors began," observed Johnny.

"Yes, rumors of possible cheating were investigated by the Department of Public Safety's Office of Professional Standards. It found that everyone in the academy class had cheated in some way by either sharing or obtaining questions and answers in an unauthorized manner."

"What happened?" asked Kelsey.

"The entire class of Georgia State Patrol troopers was fired! Every single recruit was kicked off the force. By the time the investigation ended, the recruits had completed the academy and were on the job working as state troopers. They had already written 133 speeding tickets since they graduated! Most of those violations were expected to be dismissed because the troopers who wrote them had been dismissed from the police force." (Culver, 2020; Palmer, 2019).

"Wow!" exclaimed Maria. "One 'small' unethical decision became the undoing and public humiliation of an entire class of police officers, which will affect them all into the future."

"This should be emphasized in every workplace," I observed. "Policies, codes of ethics, and regulations should emphasize how every decision and every action affects the goals and objectives of the organization and its constituents."

"So there's no way to have a smaller ethical obligation than someone else?" said Kelsey meekly.

"As human beings, we are all held to the same ethical standard," I replied. "And in the modern world, sooner or later, even your most secretive behaviors become known to those you want least to find out."

"Conduct you would not want publicly known is rarely ethical conduct," Maria remarked, "It's never something you would want to appear in the newspaper."

"Personal ethical vigilance is the only way," I concluded.

Individual responsibility and accountability

"People generally want to behave ethically." I baited the class.

"You say that most people are ethical?" asked Johnny.

"No. Most people will do the right thing when presented with a choice," I responded.

"But a significant proportion of them will not," Maria disagreed. "Rates of shoplifting, employee theft, inflated expense reports, self-dealing by public officials, all attest to this" (ACFE, 2019; Gino et al., 2011).

"Monitoring and enforcement of conduct sometimes can be taken too far---to the point where employees or citizens believe their work supervisor, or the government itself, *expects* misconduct from them," noted Johnny.

"There must exist the motivation to be honest, rather than only fear of apprehension. The likelihood of apprehension pushes people to play the odds, knowing the probability of being caught for unethical behavior is low, but the advantage to be gained worthwhile, while the rewards for being ethical are not valued," observed Maria. (see Schulze & Frank, 2003;

Wenzel, 2004).

"Did you hear about the case of the police chief in Bridgeport, Connecticut?" I asked the class.

"Bridgeport, Connecticut?" Johnny asked.

"Yes, it's the largest city in that state," replied Kelsey.

"As one of the candidates for city police chief, he received confidential information about the police chief's examination, which was stolen by the city's personnel director. This information included the questions for an upcoming oral examination and the scoring guide for required written essays for all police chief candidates. The candidate later admitted that he had two other officers complete his essays, passed the work off as his own, and lied to federal authorities in an effort to cover up his actions." I recounted.

"How could they justify doing that?" asked Maria.

"Any attempt to justify it fails every ethical test: these decisions violated several of Aristotle's moral virtues, Kant's imperatives, and Mill's principles of utilitarianism," replied Kelsey.

"But what if they thought the police chief candidate was the best person for the job?" asked Johnny.

"That sounds like arrogance to me," replied Maria. "Unethical means can never justify self-serving ends."

"Of course, there is a twist to this story," I continued. "It was alleged (but unproven) that the city personnel director was told by the mayor of the city that he wanted to be sure this particular candidate was a finalist for the position of police chief, suggesting pressure from the mayor on the city personnel director to make it happen. How does this affect the issue of moral permissibility?"

"Not at all," said Johnny and Maria simultaneously. "Pressure from a superior does not relieve your personal ethical responsibility to decline the inappropriate request, and if need be, file a whistleblower complaint, or resign from the job. That would be the ethical action to take."

"Isn't that asking a lot?" asked Kelsey.

"Yes, it is," I replied. "Remember what Aristotle said 25 centuries ago, 'anyone can get angry—that is easy—[but to act] with the right motive, and the right way, that is not for everyone, nor is it easy; wherefore goodness is both rare and laudable and noble.'" (*Nicomachean Ethics*, p. 45).

"No one is ever forced to be unethical. It's always a choice," Maria added.

"So it appears that some ethics education or training might have prevented all this," said Kelsey.

"And the failure to act with moral courage in the face of an ethical dilemma was also missing," I continued.

"What happened to them?" asked Johnny.

"Both the police chief and city personnel director were arrested and ultimately pled guilty to conspiracy to commit fraud and lying to investigators. They were also forced to resign from their jobs, pay large fines, and faced possible prison sentences (Collins, 2020).

"Staying faithful to the public interest in making government decisions lies at the core of ethical decision-making in public affairs," I concluded.

"In the private sector, the situation is similar," added Maria. "An objective accounting of possible direct or indirect harms caused by business transactions is required to ensure ethical decisions are made in manufacturing, buying, selling, and in supply chains."

Set high standards

"Vigilance is the key element of remaining ethical in your decisions," I noted.

"There is a slippery slope when unethical conduct is permitted to occur without accountability," said Maria.

"The lack of accountability creates an environment that tolerates it," added Kelsey.

"And that unethical environment makes it possible for others to act unethically," Johnny concluded.

"So every *single* act matters," I stressed.

"Leadership in institutions and agencies is needed that emphasizes the paramount importance of ethics and accountability," Maria noted.

"Training is also required to identify ethical principles, conflicts, and what to do when they arise," Kelsey added.

"Sanctions for unethical conduct must also occur to emphasize their priority to the institution, agency, or corporation," added Johnny.

"While at the same time, commendable instances of ethical decisions in difficult situations should be correspondingly rewarded," I concluded.

"So unethical conduct can be reduced, but not eliminated?" asked Johnny.

"Correct. There will always be unethical people, but removing the excuses for it through better leadership, ethics training, and sanctions, limits its spread and acceptance in both public and private life," I replied.

CHAPTER 5

Beyond the Individual:
Addressing Structural Problems

"Structural, institutional, and leadership problems have dominated global responses to unethical conduct in business and government. There is much to be said for this effort, but it does not substitute for better ethical conduct by individuals," I began the lecture.

"But doesn't the work environment play an important role?" asked Kelsey.

"Indeed it does, but the work environment does not make decisions. Only *people* make decisions, so individual thinking, training, and decision-making are what makes organizations work," I replied.

Intense workloads

"The jobs I have had in my life were crazy, with very intense workloads and unforgiving productivity goals, which resulted in the staff taking lots of unethical shortcuts," noted Maria.

"Those are structural pressures created entirely (and artificially) by management to maximize productivity, which creates unethical conduct to meet the unrealistic goals," said Johnny.

"If intense workloads are artificially created, they can be

easily eliminated through better leadership and management," responded Kelsey.

"We might add that better recruitment of staff that involves screening for ethical disposition, ethical training at the outset of employment, and regular in-service training to reflect a commitment to ethical conduct (rather than only institutional productivity goals) would also help a great deal," noted Johnny.

"There does indeed appear to be an important distinction to be made between loyalty and ethical conduct," I added. "It has been found that whistle-blowing on management misconduct is reduced when there is greater concern about loyalty over ethics---beyond one's immediate peer or workgroup." (Dunga, Young & Waytz, 2019; Nurhidayat & Kusumasari, 2019).

"Concern for others is critical to ethical action," noted Kelsey.

"Misplaced loyalty occurs when selfish or in-group focused conduct is viewed as more important than the rights or interests of others. This corrupts ethical thinking by focusing inwardly in calculating harm or advantage, rather than objectively considering others outside yourself or your in-group." I emphasized. "On a larger scale, rule of law is a concept that also connotes individual accountability under laws and regulations, as well as the application of those rules in a way that respects human rights."

"It becomes clear how concern at the individual level underlies efforts at the societal level as well, regarding the rule of law and human rights," added Johnny.

"As we have said, the approaches taken to improve the rule of law have focused largely on the structural dimensions of rule of law (e.g., transparency, impartial procedures). There has been much less attention to ethical accountability of individuals to improve decision-making to reduce selfish and self-seeking behavior, resulting in corruption, criminality, and subversion of the rule of law." Maria agreed.

"Improving ethical behavior, then, advances both public and private decision-making, leading to less reliance on the law to regulate behavior, while encouraging individual conduct in the public interest. The result will be better decisions occurring even in situations where enforcement is lacking." Kelsey concluded. (see Albanese & Artello, 2018).

Ethical Codes

"There are ethical codes in many professions and workplaces, including schools, hospitals, government agencies, and private businesses," I lectured.

"I didn't know there exists a code at this university," said Johnny.

"Oh, yes, it exists, and it has been lengthened over the years," added Maria.

"Does this mean that ethical principles have increased in number over time?" asked Kelsey.

"No, it means that selfishly motivated actors continue to find new ways to exploit them," replied Maria.

"A code of ethics is not a criminal code, and should not be book-length. It should state clear principles in actionable terms," I observed.

"Not just lists of bad acts but expected good acts as well. You get more compliance from setting expectations, and evaluating performance based on those expectations than you do simply listing what is prohibited," added Maria.

"Of course, the most important aspect of a code of ethics is creating awareness of them (via training and reminders), what happens when they are followed (visible rewards), and what occurs when they are not (visible sanctions). In this way accountability for one's ethical conduct is insured and recognized by all," I concluded.

"And what is the ultimate purpose of codes of ethics?" asked Johnny.

"*It creates a culture of integrity, which is a place where everyone would like to live and work,*" Maria recognized.

Management oversight is not enough

"The opioid epidemic that gripped multiple countries involved the invention of new, more powerful fentanyl-based pain-killers, combined with unscrupulous marketing practices," I reported.

"I heard about those cases," said Johnny. "The opioid drugs were originally developed for cancer patients whose pain could no longer be controlled with morphine. In order to expand the market for these drugs, large pharmaceutical companies had their sales forces market the drug aggressively to physicians who run pain clinics for seriously ill patients."

"They conspired to bribe the physicians in order to induce them to prescribe the fentanyl-based pain medication to patients when it was not medically necessary," said Maria.

"The bribery scheme involved sham 'speaker programs' purportedly intended to increase brand awareness of the new pain drug through educational lunches and dinners provided by physicians who used the opioids in their practice," I noted.

"Instead, the programs were actually a front with no educational component at all. They were used only as a way to pay bribes and kickbacks to targeted medical practitioners in exchange for writing more prescriptions for the drug in increased dosages," said Johnny.

"The result was non-medical use of powerful pain-killers which resulted in patient drug addiction, their job losses, family dysfunction, and death," concluded Kelsey.

"Yes, it was a culture of greed to increase profits from the powerful drugs through bribery, and then intimidation of doctors who were not prescribing enough of the drug to continue receiving 'speaker fees,'" I added.

"This sounds like an organized crime drug trafficking operation!" said Johnny.

"It was just that, only they were all white-collar professionals," observed Maria.

"So what happened to them?" asked Kelsey.

"The companies that were discovered paid large fines, a few corporate executives went to jail, but only the cases where insiders came forward could be prosecuted," I replied. (Bismuth, 2021; Kuchler et al., 2020; Laskai, 2020; U.S. Department of Justice, 2019; 2019a; 2020),

"Codes of ethics, awareness of them through training and reminders, and visible enforcement of their provisions are key elements, but leadership cannot be overlooked," I declared. "Engaged, thoughtful leadership, that is unwavering in reflecting ethical principles and practice, creates a culture in which integrity becomes a central part of your professional identity."

"Ongoing awareness, training, and enforcement breathe life into ethics codes, and makes them a centerpiece for ethical conduct in practice," Maria agreed.

"There is the human tendency to ignore, or act suspiciously of, information that contradicts your existing beliefs," Johnny noted. (Gino & Galinsky, 2012; Eil & Rao, 2011).

"So all agency guidance and directives must refer back to specific principles of ethics and integrity to make clear the moral basis for all supervision provided," added Kelsey.

"Ethical leadership rewards individuals for principled conduct, and sanctions those who violate the rules. Without it, minor ethical lapses, which are ignored, gradually become accepted conduct, and ultimately grow into larger acts of corruption." Maria concluded.

Whistleblowers

In a well-known case of police corruption, a rookie New York City Police Officer was assigned to a partner in a high-crime precinct. As a rookie, he felt powerless when his partner stole from apartments at crime scenes, and worked with drug dealers to reveal inside information about pending drug raids in exchange for cash. The rookie was further isolated when he realized that his supervisors in the precinct knew what was going on, but did nothing about it. The rookie later said, "What was I supposed to do? I was 21 years old, at the very beginning of my police career, and placed in a crime-ridden precinct with a corrupt partner and supervisors."

"This situation makes honesty extremely difficult," I remarked. "The rookie went along with the illegal and unethical conduct for several years until a drug dealer wanted him and his partner to kidnap a woman over an unpaid drug debt. At that point, the rookie contacted the internal affairs division, ultimately resulting in multiple arrests. The rookie testified in court against his partner and others." (Barer, Girardot & Eurell, 2016; *The Seven Five*, 2015).

Johnny commented on the situation, "It was a situation of a completely corrupt environment in which bribery and corruption were accepted, and police officers profited from it. It was rationalized by them because drug trafficking was widespread in the area, so rather than try to be effective as police, a number of officers decided to profit personally from it."

"It's a case where selfish conduct trumped ethical conduct," observed Maria.

←——————————————————————→

I continued, "A situation that spawned selfish conduct was made easier by pervasive corruption within the workplace. In this case, the rookie who came forward to expose the enterprise became the villain to many of those already corrupted."

"It became a case of upside-down ethics," responded Johnny.

"That must have been a rare case!" said Kelsey.

"There have been many hundreds of cases like these, documented by court cases, books, movies, and destroyed careers," I replied.

"Cases where good guys end up behaving like bad guys, and it becomes difficult to tell the difference," observed Maria.

"It reminds me of the case of Henry Hill, an organized crime figure who ended up in the witness protection program. His biography became the movie *Goodfellas*," added Johnny.

In his book, he describes his life as a young hoodlum associated with the mafia. The worldview that he and his associates held saw contempt for law-abiding citizens and those working honestly for a living.

> It was just that stuff that was stolen always tasted
> better than anything bought . . . Paulie [Vario] was
> always asking me for stolen credit cards whenever he
> and his wife, Phyllis, were going out for the night . . .
> The fact that a guy like Paul Vario, a capo in the
> Lucchese crime family, would even consider going
> out on a social occasion with his wife and run the risk
> of getting caught using a stolen credit card might

surprise some people. But if you knew wiseguys you
would know right away that the best part of the night
for Paulie came from the fact that he was getting over
on somebody . . . The real thrill of the night for Paulie,
his biggest pleasure, was that he was robbing someone
and getting away with it. (Pileggi, 1985, p.155).

"Similar to many other criminals, Hill and his associates felt
pleasure when most people properly feel guilt. In this case,
crime brought pleasure, not guilt," I remarked.

"The value system was indeed upside-down," said Maria.
"Whereas ethics focuses inculcation of moral values that
emphasize the responsibility that everyone has for his or her
decisions, there was a complete failure in this case of
individuals to comprehend, feel guilty about, or gauge their
actions by the long-term consequences of their own conduct."

"They simply didn't care about the interests or rights of
others," added Kelsey.

"Sounds like a short-hand definition of unethical conduct," I
added. "As in the case of the rookie police officer placed in a
corrupt environment, multiple ethical red flags were present
for Henry Hill: unethical leadership, no ethics education,
training or reinforcement, and no accountability for unethical
or corrupt conduct. Therefore, the reporting of this conduct
by a co-worker or associate was a rare and very risky
proposition."

"What happened to the rookie and Henry Hill?" Johnny
asked.

"The rookie ultimately avoided jail time in exchange for his testimony, but it ended his career in policing. Henry Hill also became a government witness and had to live under a new identity in a different location in the witness protection program," I replied.

"In many ways, it is surprising when whistleblowers come forward, given the career, liability, and safety risks they face," observed Kelsey.

"In most environments, speaking up against the status quo requires a strong organizational culture of integrity. The cases of the rookie and Henry Hill involved cultures that were already corrupted, making whistleblowing more difficult. The more certain an appropriate response will come from a complaint, combined with the likelihood of confidentiality, are two major considerations in reporting unethical conduct. This is especially true in the case of lower-level employees reporting on the conduct of superiors," I noted. (Devine & Maassarani, 2011; Gao & Brink, 2017; Nawawi & Salin, 2019).

* * * * * * * * *

"It's important to recognize that conduct which we often accept from private citizens somehow becomes objectionable when it is done by public officials," Johnny commented.

"Yes, public officials represent others and, therefore, should be worthy of the public trust, but the same can be said of corporate officials who are entrusted with shareholder assets, private attorneys entrusted with their clients' funds, the automobile mechanic entrusted with your car, and so on, for teachers, cooks, construction workers, and virtually all other professions," responded Maria.

"Ethics by definition involves conduct that affects others, so the public official versus private citizen distinction is probably misleading," observed Kelsey. "Instead, it is crucial to recognize that *all* unethical conduct is serious, because it affects others whose interests are equally important as fellow human beings, regardless of the social status of the wrongdoer or the victim."

"And sometimes people are refreshingly honest," I said.

"In a well-known case in New Jersey," Johnny recalled, "the mayor of a small city was opposed to approving the high-rise building development of a section of the city. A mobster, hired by a developer, visited the mayor in his apartment offering him a large cash payment for his support. The mayor turned down the offer and reported the bribe attempt to the U.S. Attorney. That took a lot of courage!" (Ross, 2014).

"Especially given that the mayor saw that the mobster in his apartment was carrying a gun inside his jacket!" added Maria.

"I believe that outraged the mayor even more," I noted.

"The mayor chose to report the incident to the U.S Attorney's Office, because he had seen in the news that office was actively pursuing corruption cases and getting convictions," Johnny indicated.

"It appears the likelihood of a serious investigation and a successful result is important in the decision to come forward with a corruption allegation," noted Maria.

"As it turns out, I see there are three groups of people," said Kelsey, "those with a strong moral identity who are unlikely to engage in self-dealing, those that will engage in unethical conduct if the circumstances are conducive, and those that are likely to engage in corrupt conduct if the likelihood of apprehension is low."

"If that is true," replied Maria, "Structural factors are needed to get the attention of the latter two groups most prone to unethical conduct, to reduce the circumstances conducive for corruption and increase the likelihood of detection."

"It looks like the mayor was in the first group: a strong moral identity that made him offended by the bribe offer," said Johnny.

"Yes, I've done many interviews with prosecutors and investigators on the subject of corruption," I replied. "None could recall another case like the mayor's." (Artello & Albanese, 2019).

"You mean to say there are not many public officials who report bribery attempts?" asked Maria sarcastically.

"You've identified the problem!" I replied.

"We need more ethical public and corporate officials who do not demand or accept bribes, combined with fewer private citizens who offer them," I concluded.

CHAPTER 6

Making it Last:
Ethical Vigilance

"The most objective, rational person you can imagine also has unconscious biases," I argued.

"Not me!" replied Johnny.

"Experiments have found that people evaluate the same facts differently; depending on their role in the situation, point of view, and other factors which do not change the facts themselves."

Maria continued the thought. "Even in otherwise clear cases of known facts, both regular people and professionals have been found to draw different conclusions." (Jordan & Meara, 1990; Nilstun & Hermeren, 2006; Shrader-Frechette, 1985).

"And we are more tolerant for our own conduct, and that of our friends, than we are of strangers --- especially strangers who are unlike us in background or culture," observed Johnny.

"It's true that when you have sympathy toward a particular person or group, you are much more likely to be lenient in your assessments of their conduct," Kelsey agreed.

"If the person is YOU, there is a strong tendency to believe your conduct is virtuous, even when it is not," added Maria.

"How do you protect against this kind of self-serving conduct?" I asked.

"You mean defending your own questionable conduct, while condemning others who do the same thing?" asked Johnny. "The best way to guard against self-serving bias is..."

"To ask your friends?" said Kelsey facetiously.

"Who are likely as biased as you are?" mocked Maria.

"Correct." I inserted. "Your friends are a bad reference point. They often have similar ethical backgrounds to you, and can be expected to be partial towards your point of view---as friends often are." (see Hildreth et al., 2016).

"It appears best to rely on ethical principles," concluded Kelsey.

"And apply them critically, so you do not find yourself relying on deceptive argumentation or information. I find that making a list on paper of the possible negative versus positive outcomes to be a useful exercise," added Maria.

"Although there is always the utilitarian propensity for weighing the outcomes in your favor. Applying the principles of ethical argument and critical thinking guard against self-serving bias." Johnny argued.

"Yes, *ethical training and critical thinking are the only way to avoid ethical blind spots*," I added. (see Bazerman &

Tenbrunsel, 2012; Sezer, Gino, & Bazerman, 2015).

"It's called ethical vigilance, and the most important person to be vigilant about is you."

"I'm reminded of the quote from the Bible," said Maria, "The highway to hell is broad, and its gate is wide for the many who choose that way. But the gateway to life is very narrow and the road is difficult, and only a few ever find it." (Matthew 7:13-14)

"The highway for unethical and corrupt conduct is also a wide road," added Kelsey.

"But the gateway to ethical conduct is not for everyone, 'nor is it easy; wherefore goodness is both rare and laudable and noble' as Aristotle said," recalled Maria.

"So we're talking about creating a major change in both private and public conduct with a cadre of individuals educated and trained on the content of ethical principles, and critical thinking exercises for applying them in practice," said Johnny.

"Individual ethical knowledge and reflection influence your behavior," Maria agreed, "but the behavior of others around you matters as well, so a corrupt culture makes ethical conduct more difficult."

"The good news is that most people want to be ethical," Kelsey offered. "They simply don't recognize ethical decisions when they appear, and don't know the principles to rely upon in making these decisions."

"This situation can be corrected through ethical education, training, moral reminders, and most of the content of this book---aimed at *preventing* unethical conduct," I added.

"Do you believe that an appeal to principles of ethics and integrity is more valid than focusing on the impact of unethical behavior on victims?" asked Johnny.

"Probably not," replied Maria. "Many corrupt decisions affect victims from a distance. For example, misspent public funds will affect paved roads, government contracts for schools and bridges, or the hiring of police officers, but these effects occur far after the corrupt act. This reduces the urgency of the perceived harm."

"When corrupt choices impact people that you likely will never meet, it becomes easier to rationalize unethical conduct," I observed.

"So an appeal to ethical principles is a stronger argument for integrity in *all* decisions, because potential outcomes are often distant and easier to dismiss?" asked Johnny.

"Yes, the good news is that most people are not psychopaths," asserted Maria.

"Psychopaths?" said Johnny with astonishment.

"You know, people who have no concern for the impact of their actions on others," replied Maria.

"I see examples in the decisions of authoritarian leaders, ruthless businesspersons, career criminals, and organized crime," observed Kelsey.

"Yes, training, monitoring, enforcement, and sanctions will always be needed to guide the actions of all of us non-psychopaths!" added Johnny.

"Remember that morals and ethics are not naturally acquired; they must be taught. There is no other source." I noted.

"We can't prevent all unethical conduct, but we can reduce it through ethics, and respond to it by holding people accountable for their actions," said Johnny.

"Pursuing cases of ethical misconduct, such as integrity violations and corruption, is what accountability really means," said Maria.

"And accountability leads to public exposure of low visibility acts," noted Kelsey.

"And that exposure leads to reform," concluded Maria.

"The lesson to be learned is that reform does not last forever," I recognized. *"The only way to ensure that ethical reform lasts is through vigilance---and vigilance involves accountability, exposure, and reform."*

* * * * * * *

"This reminds me of an exchange that took place outside of class at one of those fruit smoothie places, near the end of an ethics course," I recalled.

"Smoothie places?" repeated Johnny.

"You know, those places that put fruit and vegetables into a blender, and somehow make it taste good," I replied.

"You don't like fruit and vegetables?" asked Maria.

"I was raised on chocolate milkshakes," I attempted to defend myself, "so smoothies are a big adjustment for me."

"You should just ask them to put some chocolate into your smoothie," noted Kelsey.

"Are you allowed to do that?" I asked with astonishment.

"It's all fair game in the land of smoothies!" added Johnny.

While we were out enjoying our smoothies, I said, "Here's something you ought to be thinking about, especially at the end of a course about ethics: what *should* I be doing with my life?"

"That is to say, it's time to ask yourself the most important question of all: *What am I actually doing with all my decisions and activity throughout my life?*"

"I'm working, playing, paying bills, commuting, being late for appointments, and never quite keeping up with my social commitments," replied Johnny.

"Is it frantic?" I asked.

"Yes, that's a good word for it," said Johnny.

"But what is its meaning?" asked Maria.

"It's *meaning*?" Johnny asked.

←——————————————————————→

"Yes, what was the real purpose of all that activity, other than keeping busy enough to keep all the balls in the air?" added Kelsey.

"Balls in the air?" said Johnny.

"You know, working, playing, paying bills, commuting, being late for appointments, and never quite keeping up with your social commitments," replied Kelsey.

"Well, that was pretty much all of it," answered Johnny.

"Don't you envision a future for yourself beyond your present situation?" asked Maria.

"You mean retirement?" said Johnny with surprise.

"No, retirement is simply choosing not to work as much as you once did, in order to keep paying your bills, commute less often, play, be late for appointments, and never quite keeping up with your social commitments," I inserted.

"You're asking me to consider what is it that gives my life meaning?" Johnny asked again.

"Yes, what gives your life meaning at this, *or any,* moment?" asked Maria.

"I try not to think about that. I never had much time to think about it, and even if I did, I'm afraid of what the answer might be," said Johnny meekly.

"Maybe it's time to challenge yourself to make some personal changes," observed Kelsey.

I added, "Concentration camp survivor Victor Frankl (1946) said it best when he stated that everything can be taken from you, except "the last of the human freedoms: *to choose one's attitude in any given set of circumstances, to choose one's own way.*"

"So I can *choose* to define myself to be a victim of life, an unhappy employed or unemployed worker, or a disease carrier?" asked Johnny.

"Or a global citizen, a lover of all people, a helper to others less fortunate," responded Maria. "Only *you* decide your attitude and what will become of you as a person,"

"Well, I'm a little confused about my life's purpose with that kind of pressure! Do you have any suggestions?" Johnny said hesitantly.

"Yes, I do," I replied. "Reading about the lives and ideas of others from the past, combined with lots of your personal experience from the present, leads to one conclusion."

"And what's that?" asked Johnny.

"There's only one way to give your life actual meaning, beyond just staying busy."

"How do I get actual meaning from life?" asked Johnny incredulously.

"*Your living only has meaning to the extent you are living for other,.*" I responded.

"But what about my *own* life?" asked Johnny.

"You can certainly choose to achieve personal goals, but if you're doing it only for yourself, it's an empty experience that will quickly be forgotten by almost everyone, once you're gone," Maria observed.

"Living for others ---doing things that have an impact on the lives of others --- is the only thing that gives life meaning. And it's the only way to show love or live ethically," added Kelsey.

"But what about working, playing, paying bills, commuting, being late for appointments, and never quite keeping up with my social commitments?" asked Johnny.

"That stuff keeps you *busy*, but it doesn't provide *meaning*. It has meaning only when you are doing it so that your effort is carried out for the benefit of others --- friends, family, patients, students, clients, or society in general," I replied.

"There is no other way to achieve a life of meaning?" Johnny asked again.

"Your life has meaning to the extent you're living for others." I concluded.

"It's that simple?" said Johnny.

"And you love to the extent you're living for others," Kelsey added.

"It's always been that simple. You've just become distracted working, playing, paying bills, commuting, being late for appointments, and never quite keeping up with your social commitments!"

"Ethics provides the way to see that there is a greater purpose to life than self-interest," Kelsey concluded.

"Living with respect and caring deeply about the interests of others is central to the quest for consistent ethical conduct," I added.

"And the only way to ensure that ethical reform lasts is through vigilance," added Maria. "And vigilance involves personal accountability, exposure, and reform."

Johnny added, "I think I should go back and read this book from the beginning."

"If it improves your ethical outlook, it is time well spent," Kelsey and Maria replied in unison.

"Think for a moment about what will be said about you when you die," I asked my class to think. "Write what you might wish to appear on your tombstone."

"Well, that certainly helps you clarify and prioritize ethical principles in life," said Johnny.

"Yes, words like 'character' and 'values' and 'caring' seem to be much more important in that context, than do achievement, wealth, or success," Maria added.

"Consider the story of Alfred Nobel," I continued. "He was a chemist best known for inventing dynamite. His brother died while Alfred was still alive, and the newspaper mistakenly printed Alfred's obituary instead of his brother's. It was that rare case of being able to read your own obituary while you are still alive."

"He read the obituary that saluted him as the inventor of dynamite (perhaps the most destructive explosive of his time) and described how he made a lot of money in the process. He was horrified by his obituary, and resolved to establish a different legacy."

"What did he do?" asked Kelsey.

"He gave away his wealth and established the Nobel Prize for achievement in various fields of endeavor that contribute to society in general," I replied.

"What will be said about you in *your* obituary?

"If you want to know how to live your life, think about what you'd like people to say about you after you die — then live backwards."

"Your ethics begins with your next decision."

References

5th Pillar. (2020). *Zero Rupee Note: A Non-Violent Weapon of Non-Cooperation Against Corruption.* https://5thpillar.org/programs/zero-rupee-note/ (accessed June 2020).

ACFE. (2019). *Report to the Nations: 2018 Global Study on Occupational Fraud and Abuse.* Association of Certified Fraud Examiners. https://s3-us-west-2.amazonaws.com/acfepublic/2018-report-to-the-nations.pdf

Albanese, J.S. & Artello, K. (2018). Focusing Anti-Corruption Efforts More Effectively: An Empirical Look at Offender Motivation -- Positive, Classical, Structural and Ethical Approaches. *Advances in Applied Sociology*, vol.8, 471-485.

Aquino, K. & Reed, A. (2002). The Self-Importance of Moral Identity. *Journal of Personality and Social Psychology*, vol. 83, 1423-1440.

Aristotle. (1925). *The Nicomachean Ethics.* (340 B.C.) Oxford University Press.

Artello, K. & Albanese, J.S. (2019). The Calculus of Public Corruption Cases: Hidden Decisions in Investigations and Prosecutions. *Journal of Criminal Justice and Law,* vol. 3, 21-36.

Barer, Burl, Franck C. Girardot, Jr., & Ken Eurell. (2017). *Betrayal in Blue: The Shocking Memoir of the Scandal That Rocked the NYPD.* Wildblue Press.

Barry, V. (1998). *The Dog Ate My Homework: Personal Responsibility—How We Avoid It and What to Do about It.* New York: Andrews McMeel.

Bazerman, M.H., & Tenbrunsel, A.E. (2012). *Blind Spots: Why We Fail to Do What's Right and What to Do about It.* Princeton University Press.

Bismuth, C. (2021). *Bad Medicine: Catching New York's Deadliest Pill Pusher.* Atria/One Signal Publishers.

Bok, S. (1999*). Lying: Moral Choice in Public and Private Life.* New York: Vintage Books.

Borgman, A. (1995). Massage Parlor Raids: Did Police Cross The Line? *The Washington Post*, October 13.

Bursztyn, L., Fiorin, S. Gottlieb, D, & Janz, M. (2015). Moral Incentives in Credit Card Debt Repayment: Evidence from a Field Experiment. *NBER Working Papers, 21611.* National Bureau of Economic Research.

Collins, D. (2020). Police Chief, City Official Plead Guilty in Hiring Scam. *Associated Press*, October 5.

Culver, J. (2020). 'A punch in the gut': Georgia State Patrol Troopers Fired after Investigation into Cheating Allegations. *USA Today*, January 29.

Devine, TR. & Maassarani, T.F. (2011). *The Corporate Whistleblowers Survival Guide: A Handbook for Committing the Truth.* Berrett-Koehler Publishers.

Dunga, J.S., Young, L. & Waytz, A. (2019). The Power of Moral Concerns in Predicting Whistleblowing Decisions. *Journal of Experimental Social Psychology*, vol. 85, 1-12.

Eil, D. & Rao, J. (2011). The Good News-Bad News Effect: Asymmetric Processing of Objective Information about

Yourself. *American Economic Journal: Microeconomics*, vol. 3, 114-138.

Facione, P. (1990). *Critical Thinking: A Statement of Expert Consensus for Purposes of Educational Assessment and Instruction.* California Academic Press.

Falk, A. & Kosfeld, M. (2006). The Hidden Costs of Control. *American Economic Review*, vol. 96, 1611-1630.

Falk, A. & Szech, N. (2013). Organizations, Diffused Pivotality and Immoral Outcomes. *IZA Discussion Paper* No. 7442. Available at SSRN: https://ssrn.com/abstract=2283557

Fellner, G., Sausgruber, R., & Traxler, C. (2013). Testing Enforcement Strategies in the Field: Threat, Moral Appeal and Social Information. *Journal of the European Economic Association,* vol. 11, 634-660.

Frankl, V. (2006). *Man's Search for Meaning.* (1946) Beacon Press.

Gao, L. & Brink, A.G. (2017). Whistleblowing Studies in Accounting Research: A Review of Experimental Studies on the Determinants of Whistleblowing. *Journal of Accounting Literature*, vol.38, 1-13.

Gino, F., Schweitzer, M.E., Mead, N .L. & Ariely, D. (2011). Unable to Resist Temptation: How Self-control Depletion Promotes Unethical Behavior. *Organizational Behavior and Human Decision Processes*, Vol. 115,191-203.

Gino, F. & Galinsky, A. (2012). Vicarious Dishonesty: When Psychological Closeness Creates Distance from One's Moral

Compass. *Organizational Behavior and Human Decision Processes*, vol. 119, 15-26.

Goldstein, S. (2013). Cops in Florida Bare it all during Massage Parlor Prostitution Sting. *New York Daily News*, April 21.

Gourevitch, P. (1999). *We Wish to Inform You That Tomorrow We Will be Killed with Our Families: Stories from Rwanda.* Picador.

Grym, J. & Liljander, V. (2016). To Cheat or Not to Cheat? The Effect of a Moral Reminder on Cheating. *Nordic Journal of Business*, vol. 65, 18-37.

Hamman, J., Lowenstein, G. & Weber, R. (2010). Self-Interest through Delegation: An Additional Rationale for the Principal-Agent Relationship. *American Economics Review*, vol. 100, 1826-1846.

Handelman, S. (2019). A Detective's Worst Foe: 'Flawed Thinking.' *Thecrimereport.org*, November 15.

Hicken, A., Leider, S., Ravanilla, N, & Yang, D. (2015). Measuring Vote-Selling: Field Evidence from the Philippines. *American Economic Review*, vol. 105, 352-356.

Hildreth, J., Gino, F., & Bazerman, N. (2016). Blind Loyalty? When Group Loyalty Makes Us See Evil or Engage in It. *Organizational Behavior and Human Decision Processes*, vol. 132, 16-36.

Hill, C., Memon, A., & McGeorge, P. (2008). The Role of Confirmation Bias in Suspect Interviews: A Systematic

Evaluation. *Legal & Criminological Psychology*, vol. 13, 357-371.

Ilibagiza, I. (2007). *Left to Tell: One Woman's Story of Surviving the Rwandan Genocide*. Hay House Publishers.

Isakov, M. & Tripathy, A. (2017). Behavioral Correlates of Cheating: Environmental Specificity and Reward Expectation. *PLoS ONE*. vol. 12, October 26, 1-12.

Jordan, A. E., & Meara, N. M. (1990). Ethics and the Professional Practice of Psychologists: The role of virtues and principles. *Professional Psychology: Research and Practice*, vol. 21, 107-114.

Kahana, B., Kahana, E., Harel, Z. & Segal, M. (1985). The Victim as Helper: Prosocial Behavior during the Holocaust. *Humbolt Journal of Social Relations*, vol. 13, 357-373.

Kant, I. (1993). *Grounding for the Metaphysics of Morals*. (1785). Hackett Publishing.

Kidder, R.M. (1996). *How Good People Make Tough Choices*. New York: Simon & Schuster.

Kuchler, H., Connaire, S., Verbitsky, N., Wong, A., Blandon, R., & Jennings, T. (2020). *Opioids, Bribery and Wall Street: The Inside Story of a Disgraced Drugmaker*. https://www.pbs.org/wgbh/frontline/article/opioid-drugmaker-insys-bribing-doctors-fentanyl-painkiller/ June 18.

Laskai, A. (2020). *Institutional Corruption Theory in Pharmaceutical Industry-Medicine Relationships*. Springer.

Lowenstein, G. (1993). Self-serving Assessments of Fairness and Pretrial Bargaining. *Journal of Legal Studies*, vol. 22,

135-159.

Messner, M. (2020). *The Ethics of Encounter*. Orbis Books.

Mill, John Stuart. (1993). *Utilitarianism*. (1863). Prometheus Books.

Nawawi, A. & Salin, A.S. (2019).To Whistle or Not to Whistle? Determinants and Consequences. *Journal of Financial Crime*, vol. 26, 260-276.

Nilstun, T. & Hermeren, G. (2006). Human Tissue Samples and Ethics. *Medicine, Health Care and Philosophy*, vol. 9, 81-86.

Nurhidayat, I. & Kusumasari, B. (2019). Why would Whistleblowers Dare to Reveal Wrongdoings? An Ethical Challenge and Dilemma for Organisations. *International Journal of Law and Management*, vol. 61, 505-515.

OECD. (2018). *Behavioural In sights for Public Integrity: Harnessing the Human Factor to Counter Corruption*. Paris: Organisation for Economic Cooperation and Development.

Palmer, C. (2019). Philly Police: 10 recruits resigned after trying to cheat on open-book test, *The Philadelphia Inquirer*, June 24.

Pileggi, Nicholas. (1985). *Wiseguy: Life in a Mafia Family*. Simon & Schuster.

Plato. (1980). *Meno*. (ca. 385 B.C.) Indianapolis: Hackett Publishing,

Plato. (1994). *The Republic*. (ca. 370 B.C.) New York: Oxford University Press.

Power, S. (2001). Bystanders to Genocide. *The Atlantic*,

September.

Pruckner, G. & Sausgruber, R. (2013). Honesty on the Streets: A Field Study on Newspaper Purchasing. *Journal of the European Economic Association*, vol. 11, 661-679.

Raghavan, S. (2014). Rwandans Mark 20th Anniversary of Genocide amid Reminders that Justice has yet to be Done. *The Washington Post*, April 7.

Ross, Philip. (2014). *The Bribe*. Open Road Distribution.

Roth, M.S. (2010). Beyond Critical Thinking. *Chronicle of Higher Education*, vol. 56, January 8, B4.

Rubin D.C. (2014). How Quickly We Forget. *Science*, vol. 346, November, 1058-9.

Sabalow, R. (2013). Experts Question Police Methods in Carmel and Zionsville Prostitution Sting. *Indystar.com*, May 3.

Schulz, G. & Frank, B. (2003). Deterrence versus Intrinsic Motivation: Experimental Evidence on the Determinants of Corruptibility. *Economics of Governance*, vol. 4, 143-160.

Schumacher-Matos, E. (2008). "Fake-Brands Story Needed More Discretion," *Miami Herald*, February 3.

Sezer, O., Gino, F., & Bazerman, M. (2015). Ethical Blind Spots: Explaining Unintentional Unethical Behavior. *Current Opinion in Psychology*, vol. 6, 77-81.

Shapiro, S. (2010). Decision Making Under Pressure. *The Futurist*, vol. 44, January-February, 42.

Shrader-Frechette, K. (1985). *Risk Analysis and Scientific Method: Methodological and Ethical Problems with*

Evaluating Societal Hazards. Reidel Publishing.

Staub, E. (2003). *The Psychology of Good and Evil: Why Children, Adults, and Groups Help and Harm Others.* London: Cambridge University Press.

Students and Course Content: How Fast Do They Forget? (2007). *Teaching Professor*, vol. 21, Issue 7, 2.

Tarrant. M. (2012). Social Identity and Perceptions of Torture: It's Moral When We Do It. *Journal of Experimental Psychology*, vol. 48, 513-518.

Thaler, R.H. & Sunstein, C.R. (2009). *Nudge: Improving Decisions about Health, Wealth, and Happiness.* Penguin Books.

The Seven Five. (2015). Movie, directed by T. Russell.

U.S. Department of Justice. (2019). *Founder and Four Executives of Insys Therapeutics Convicted of Racketeering Conspiracy.* Office of Public Affairs. May 2.

U.S. Department of Justice. (2019a). *Pharmaceutical Company Targeting Elderly Victims Admits to Paying Kickbacks.* Office of Public Affairs. September 26.

U.S. Department of Justice. (2020). *Former CEO of Insys Therapeutics Sentenced for Racketeering Scheme.* Office of Public Affairs. January 22.

Vigdor, N. (2020). Tennessee Brothers Who Hoarded Hand Sanitizer Settle to Avoid Price-Gouging Fine. *The New York Times*, April 22.

Visser-Wijnveen, G.J., J.H. Van Driel, R.M. Van der Rijst, N. Verloop, A. Visser. (2009).The Relationship between Academics' Conceptions of Knowledge, Research and

Teaching – A Metaphor Study. *Teaching in Higher Education*, vol. 14, December, 673.

Wenzel, M. (2004). The Social Side of Sanctions: Personal and Social Norms as Moderators of Deterrence. *Law & Human Behavior*, vol. 28, 547–567.

World Bank. (2015). *Mind, Society, and Behavior.* Washington, DC: World Bank.

ABOUT THE AUTHOR

Jay S. Albanese is professor in the Wilder School of Government & Public Affairs at Virginia Commonwealth University. He was the first Ph.D. recipient from the School of Criminal Justice at Rutgers University. Dr. Albanese served as Chief of the International Center at the National Institute of Justice, the research arm of the U.S. Department of Justice.

Dr. Albanese is author and editor of 22 books including *My Search for Meaning: A Professor, His Students, and 12 Great Conversations* (McMaster Media, 2020), *Organized Crime: From the Mob to Transnational Organized Crime* (Routledge, 2015), *Transnational Crime & the 21st Century: Criminal Enterprise, Corruption, and Opportunity* (Oxford, 2011), and he is editor-in-chief of the 5-volume *Encyclopedia of Criminology & Criminal Justice* (Wiley, 2014).

Dr. Albanese is recipient of the ***Distinguished Teaching Award*** from Virginia Commonwealth University, the ***Gerhard Mueller Award*** for research contributions from the Academy of Criminal Justice Sciences International Section, and the ***Distinguished Scholar Award*** from the International Association for the Study of Organized Crime. He is a past president and fellow of the Academy of Criminal Justice Sciences, and is co-founder of Criminologists without Borders. *www.jayalbanese.com*

---

www.ingramcontent.com/pod-product-compliance
Lightning Source LLC
LaVergne TN
LVHW020800070125
800695LV00002B/139

* 9 7 8 1 7 3 3 3 0 0 4 2 1 *